TEXAS OBLIVION

MYSTERIOUS DISAPPEARANCES, ESCAPES AND COVER-UPS

E.R. BILLS

THE
History
PRESS

Published by The History Press
Charleston, SC
www.historypress.com

First published 2021

Manufactured in the United States

ISBN 9781467147378

Library of Congress Control Number: 2020951651

For the lost and their loved ones.

CONTENTS

CONTENTS

PREFACE

I n his last known piece of correspondence before he vanished in El Paso in December 1913, American writer Ambrose Bierce was ominous. "As to me," he wrote, "I leave here tomorrow for an unknown destination."

It was unknown to him and us, as it turns out. And that will probably always be the case.

The mystery behind Bierce's disappearance has been wrestled with for over a century but never satisfactorily resolved. His fate is a question mark. We're left with only rumor and speculation. But Bierce was not the first or the last person to go missing in Texas—his date with oblivion just generated the most interest and fanfare.

This book is devoted to some of the rest. It doesn't cover all of the mysterious disappearances in Texas, but it explores several of the unsolved incidents before 1990 and one bizarre case in 1992. The lost deserve to have their stories told. Their friends, loved ones and descendants should see them remembered and someday maybe even recovered.

Until then, here are clues about some of their fates.

E.R.

1
VOYAGE TO OBLIVION

On Saturday, February 2, 1963, Edith Martin kissed her husband, Adam, before he climbed aboard the SS *Marine Sulphur Queen* in Beaumont, Texas. A forty-seven-year-old third engineer, Adam was one of the last crewmen to walk up the gangway, and Edith, forty-four, was the last loved one to watch the 524-foot, 7,240-ton tanker depart. She had at least a three-hour drive back to their home in Austin, but it was still relatively early. She stood at the wharf for a long while, watching the *Sulphur Queen* pass out of sight.

In the years to come, Edith was glad she lingered. She was the last one to see any crew member of the ill-fated *Marine Sulphur Queen*, alive or dead.

ORIGINALLY PART OF THE Fast Tanker Operation in World War II, the T2-SE-A1 *Marine Sulphur Queen* was first christened the SS *Esso New Haven* and used for oil transport. In 1960, it was converted into a molten sulphur[1] carrier by the Bethlehem Steel Company in Maryland. The conversion involved reconfiguring a number of the original holds to create a special, independent tank (over three hundred feet in length), which was internally separated into four smaller holds. The installation, which retrofitted the *Sulphur Queen* to transport molten sulphur kept at a temperature of 265 degrees Fahrenheit, necessitated modifying the internal structure of the vessel and the removal of all traverse bulkheads. The *Sulphur Queen* was the first T2 tanker converted for this type of specialized cargo, and the scheduled five-day voyage—beginning on February 2—to Norfolk,

Virginia, was to be its sixty-fourth, inching it ever closer to the one-million-ton mark of molten sulphur portage.

Laden with over fifteen thousand tons on this trip, the 7,200-horsepower turboelectric vessel cleared the Sabine Bar sea buoy at 6:00 p.m. (CST). A day and a half later, on February 4 at 1:24 a.m. (EST), the *Marine Sulphur Queen* sent a regular radio message indicating its position as approximately 360 miles south of Panama City, Florida, and 200 miles off Key West (25°45'N, 86°W). At 11:23 a.m. (EST), two unsuccessful attempts to contact the *Sulphur Queen* were made from the mainland. At that point, the estimated position of the vessel was approximately twenty miles due west of the Dry Tortugas and eighty-five miles from Key West (24°40'N, 83°19'W).

When the *Marine Sulphur Queen* didn't arrive at Norfolk on February 7, it was reported missing and searches began. Coast Guard planes from New Orleans, Miami and Virginia joined the hunt, and an early sighting raised hopes, but they were quickly dashed. The pilot of a low-flying aircraft had spotted a ship matching the *Sulphur Queen*'s description, the first word in the name being "Marine" and the last appearing to be "Queen"—but the middle name was smudged. It turned out to be the *Marine Dow Chem*, a sister ship operated by the same company, Marine Transport Lines Inc.

Recent weather conditions along the southeastern coast increased anxieties regarding the *Marine Sulphur Queen*'s fate. The overdue tanker had apparently encountered twenty-five- to fifty-mile-per-hour winds and fourteen to twenty-foot seas. But one Coast Guard spokesman said that that was a misnomer, because ships like the *Sulphur Queen* sit low in the water. "To a tanker, a 14-foot sea is like a 28-foot sea to any other ship."

The Port Houston Coast Guard commander, Commodore E.T. Sawyer, was skeptical. "I don't think a vessel of her size is in any serious trouble," he said. "Any number of things could have happened." Lieutenant Richard Westcott, the duty officer for the Coast Guard station in Portsmouth, Virginia, concurred. He maintained that there was no reason to "fear any disaster" yet, but they weren't taking any chances. "We have had an all ships broadcast out since last night," Westcott said, "requesting sightings or knowledge of the vessel from any other ship at sea. So far, we have heard nothing." The families of those aboard the *Marine Sulphur Queen* subsequently received the following Western Union telegram: "Marine sulphur queen scheduled arrive norfolk afternoon 7th unreported and overdue stop coast guard and ships endeavoring communicate with and locate vessel stop we also doing everything possible and we will keep you closely advised marine transport lines inc."

The freighter SS *Marine Sulphur Queen* at dock. *Courtesy of the* Green Bay Gazette.

A list of the missing *Marine Sulphur Queen* merchant seamen was posted in newspapers on February 10, 1963. The officers included Captain James V. Fanning, Beaumont; chief mate George E. Watson, Galveston; second mate Henry Hall, Beaumont; third mate Frank Cunningham, Beaumont; radio officer George Sloat, Baltimore; boatswain Evans Phillips, Tampa Bay; and chief engineer Leon Clauser, Beaumont. The rest of the crew included John Ardoin of Beaumont; Everett Arnold of Memphis; Fred A. Bodden of Philadelphia; James Bodden of Tampa Bay; Henry Clark of Jersey City, New Jersey; Ceburn R. Cole of Lake Charles, Louisiana; Leroy Courville of Groves, Texas; Nelaton Devine of Port Arthur; Charles Dorsey of New York; Wesley Fontenot of Manou, Louisiana; Leroy Green of Rahway, New Jersey; John Grice of Daytona Beach; Robert Harold of Norfolk, Virginia; Aaron Heard of Norfolk, Virginia; Hugh Hunter of Chapel Hill, North Carolina; John Husch Jr. of Akron, Ohio; third assistant engineer Adam Martin of Austin; Willie Mauel of Ville Platte, Louisiana; Clarence McGuire of Bronson, Texas; John Nieznajski of Gary, Indiana; James Phillips of Port Arthur; Walter Pleasant of Port Arthur; Warren Santos of Newark, New Jersey; third assistant engineer Eugene W. Schneeberger of Beaumont; Cornelius Smith of Port Arthur;

Althan Tate of Philadelphia; chief cook Vincent Thompson of Baltimore; Alejandro Valdez of Port Arthur; second assistant engineer Albert Van Sickle of Baltimore; first assistant engineer John Venton of Friendswood, Texas; and Jesse Vicera of Linden, New Jersey.

Some compared the *Marine Sulphur Queen*'s disappearance to that of the USS *Cyclops* in 1918. The *Cyclops* had disembarked from Rio de Janeiro, Brazil, and stopped for coal in Barbados. Headed for Baltimore, the vessel was carrying a crew of 309 and a cargo of manganese. It disappeared just like the *Sulphur Queen*.

Others believed the *Marine Sulphur Queen* and its crew were "hijacked" and taken to Havana. The Cuban Missile Crisis[2] had occurred only a few months earlier. The Coast Guard asked the U.S. State Department to check unconfirmed reports that the *Sulphur Queen* was taken to Cuba.

One navy patrol plane spotted a swathe of "yellow substance" near Jacksonville, Florida, and assumed it might be the result of sulphur spillage, but a closer examination revealed it was a tidal accumulation of seaweed and flotsam. An officer at the Jacksonville Coast Guard station expressed frustration. "We're undoubtedly looking for the remains of a sea disaster," he said. "It could have blown up or broken up and sunk without a survivor. Or maybe it was hijacked. God knows where the tanker is now."

State Department spokesperson Lincoln White said that the Cubans, who had been contacted through Swiss emissaries, claimed to know nothing about *Marine Sulphur Queen*'s whereabouts but promised to forward any information that might become available on the vessel. White conceded that no one had solid information on the ship's fate.

The massive aerial search, which extended over two dozen miles on each side of the track line of the *Marine Sulphur Queen*'s estimated route, lasted five days and was composed of eighty-three sorties covering approximately 350,000 square miles of the Gulf of Mexico and the Atlantic Ocean. No trace of the *Sulphur Queen* was discovered, and the thirty-nine crewmen's families received a second Western Union telegram from Marine Transport Lines on Valentine's Day. It informed them that the Coast Guard search had been discontinued and that the evidence thus far indicated a "probable loss" of the *Sulphur Queen* and its crew.

The families of the crewmen, however, remained hopeful. Mark Fanning, the sixteen-year-old son of the ship's captain, James W. Fanning, was unfazed. "My dad's the greatest," he said. "He's had close calls before. He loves the sea, and it will never defeat him." A close Fanning family friend was also confident. "Jim has been on the sea in everything that will float—he has

Coast Guard lieutenant William Troutman with one of the recovered *Marine Sulphur Queen* life jackets. *Courtesy of the* Record *(Hackensack, New Jersey).*

faced danger many times and come through all right—we feel this time will not be an exception."

On February 16, 1963, *Marine Sulphur Queen* regular second mate David E. Fike, who passed on the tanker's latest voyage to extend his vacation, said he was surprised at the cessation in radio communication because the *Sulphur Queen* had two high-frequency transmitters with emergency batteries and a radio telephone. "The radio silence is the thing that's got me stumped," he remarked. On February 18, a Coast Guard Board of Inquiry regarding the *Marine Sulphur Queen*'s disappearance began in Beaumont, and five of the crew members' wives filed a $2.5 million federal lawsuit claiming that their

Ada Heard holds up her one-year-old son, Kim. Kim's father, Aaron, vanished with the rest of the crew of the *Marine Sulphur Queen. Courtesy of* Green Bay Gazette.

husbands lost their lives because the tanker was "unsafe, unseaworthy and improperly loaded."

On February 20, 1963, a Coast Guard cutter retrieved two *Marine Sulphur Queen* life jackets, a lifeboat megaphone and some board fragments twelve miles southwest of Key West. The cutter commander, Tom Troutman of Knoxville, believed the equipment had been in the water for at least a week, because the items were already showing marine growth. Troutman also noted that the life preservers could have drifted 275 miles southeast in that time span. The recovered wood fragments showed no sign of fire damage.

The aerial search for the *Marine Sulphur Queen* recommenced, this time focusing on the eastern edge of the Gulf of Mexico, the Bahamas and the Straits of Florida. The navy also began an underwater search for the vessel.[3] On February 21, a helicopter pilot searching for *Sulphur Queen* survivors discovered one of the tanker's life rings with a man's jacket attached to it in shark-infested waters near Fowey Rocks Lighthouse, six miles southeast of Miami. And another *Sulphur Queen* life ring was discovered by a different search crew twenty miles away. Meanwhile, at the Coast Guard hearing in Beaumont, Gene Merryman, who occasionally served as a relief third mate on the tanker, testified that the *Queen* suffered weather damage in recent storms and had been plagued by small fires and noxious sulphur fumes and was due for drydock maintenance and overhaul soon.

On Wednesday, February 26, Fike testified that the *Marine Sulphur Queen* had run aground twice in Tampa Bay since it began transporting sulphur but that a tugboat pilot was in control of the ship both times. Fike also said that the *Sulphur Queen*'s biennial inspection to determine the vessel's seaworthiness was scheduled for January 30, but it had been postponed. When pressed about why the *Sulphur Queen*'s inspection was postponed, Fike said the Texas Gulf Sulphur Company was running behind on its orders of molten sulphur and needed the tanker in service.

The families of the thirty-nine men believed to be lost on the *Marine Sulphur Queen* began receiving insurance payments of $7,000 to $10,000[4] on

Tuesday, March 5, 1963. Assorted life preservers and other items from the *Sulphur Queen* continued to turn up intermittently, but the vessel itself was never found, and all search efforts were halted again on March 14, 1963.

By late March 1963, the Coast Guard was conducting the Board of Inquiry in New York, and Edward P. Rahe, the technical superintendent of the team that retrofitted the *Marine Sulphur Queen* for sulphur transport, testified that he didn't think sulphur leakage would have seriously damaged the *Sulphur Queen* but that he was unable to explain the vessel's disappearance. Tankers like the *Sulphur Queen* operating under similar circumstances had weathered structural compromise and vessel breakup before and continued to float or hold together well enough to be towed into port.[5]

In April 1963, a message in a bottle purported to have been placed in the ocean by a *Marine Sulphur Queen* seaman turned up one thousand miles away, near Corpus Christi. Composed on brown paper and sealed in a whiskey bottle, one side read, "S.O.S. Sulfur [*sic*] Queen. Help!" The other side read, "Our ship was sailing steadily. Suddenly there was an explotion [*sic*]. Two men were hurt. That is all I have to say because I am getting—"

Most experts believed it was hardly possible that the bottle could have traveled as far as Corpus Christi but admitted it was plausible if the bottle was propelled by several days of strong winds. An Internal Revenue

Some people believed the *Marine Sulphur Queen* had been seized and delivered into the hands of Che Guevara and Fidel Castro. *Courtesy of the Museo Che Guevara in Havana, Cuba.*

Service handwriting specialist studied the short missive and records of crew correspondence and concluded that the handwriting belonged to crewman Walter J. Pleasant.

In the course of the Coast Guard hearings, it was learned that two American merchantmen saw the *Marine Sulphur Queen* twenty-five miles southwest of the Dry Tortugas flying a *not under command* signal on February 4, 1963. A not under command signal is communicated by two black balls suspended vertically, one beneath the other, on a halyard on the deck of a vessel. It is universally understood to not be a request for assistance or a plea for help—simply a visual status report. This was apparently the last known sighting of the vessel, and experts assumed it sank that day.

By March 1964, the disappearance of the *Marine Sulphur Queen* was being referred to as a "voyage to oblivion."[6] On Monday, April 13, 1964, the Coast Guard Board of Inquiry concluded that the tanker capsized and sank off the Atlantic coast of Florida after an explosion or structural collapse. Since no distress signal was apparently sent out or received, it was assumed that the ship sank quickly, and the board recommended that no further T2-SE-A1 tankers be converted to molten sulphur transports.

ON DECEMBER 5, 1945—ALMOST three months to the day after World War II ended—a group of five Grumman TBM Avenger torpedo bombers (later dubbed Flight 19 but also known as the Lost Patrol) disappeared during an overwater navigation training exercise just east of Florida. All fourteen airmen participating in the exercise were lost, and they were soon joined by the thirteen-man crew of the Martin PBM Mariner flying boat that was launched from Naval Air Station Banana River (now known as Patrick Air Force Base) to locate them. The PBM aircraft was notorious for accumulating fuel vapors in its bilges, and investigators believed that the PBM Mariner probably exploded mid-flight while searching for the Lost Patrol. The navy never solved the disappearance of Flight 19, and no traces of the TBM Avengers or the PBM flying boat or their crew members has ever been found.

In an article titled "Sea Mystery at Our Back Door" in the October 1952 issue of *Fate* magazine,[7] writer George X. Sand discussed the strange number of air and sea disappearances that had occurred in "a watery triangle bounded roughly by Florida, Bermuda and Puerto Rico." In the piece, he discussed the bizarre details of Flight 19 and the mysterious disappearances of the *Star Ariel* (an Avro Tudor Mark IVB passenger aircraft operated by British South American Airways) on January 17, 1949, and the SS *Sandra* in 1950 (a 350-foot-long American freighter), among others. By the early 1960s, Sand's "watery triangle" had become known as the "Deadly Triangle." But the moniker didn't pinpoint the area geographically. This changed when paranormal writer Vincent H. Gaddis referred to Sand's "watery triangle" as the "Deadly Bermuda Triangle" in the cover story of the February 1964 issue of *Argosy* magazine.[8] The article discussed more recent disappearances, including the details regarding the fate of the *Marine Sulphur Queen*.

As previously noted, on Monday, April 13, 1964—almost as if in response to Gaddis's article in *Argosy*—the Coast Guard Board of Inquiry concluded that the *Marine Sulphur Queen* capsized and sank off the east coast of Florida

A patrol of five Grumman TBM Avengers similar to the ones that disappeared into the Bermuda Triangle in 1945. *Courtesy of the National Archives and Records Administration.*

after an explosion or structural collapse. The possible causes the report listed for the loss of the ship included an explosion in the cargo tanks; failure of the hull girder, which would have caused the tanker to break in two; a huge wave that might have capsized the vessel; or a steam explosion.

In a March 9, 1969 story in the *Chicago Tribune*, John Godwin referred to the "Deadly Bermuda Triangle" as the "Hoodoo Sea" and examined the possibility that the disappearance of the *Marine Sulphur Queen* was a result of a "freak sea":

> *Some scientists have advanced the theory of the freak sea, a single mountainous wave of fantastic proportions that has been known to engulf large ships. Riding up to 100 feet or more, such a salt water Everest[9] can catch a vessel square on the beam, can cause a well-secured cargo to slide, thus rolling the craft over within less than a minute. In such an accident, there would be no time to radio nor to launch a lifeboat.*

In June 1969, John Wallace Spencer published *Limbo of the Lost*, the first book devoted to the disappearances and strange phenomena in the Triangle. He examined the *Marine Sulphur Queen* case extensively and gave the "freak sea" theory short shrift, but his notes about the one condition that every expert and investigating party seemed to agree on were interesting:

> *Seamen familiar with the missing tanker testified that ships like the* Queen *just didn't go down very fast, at least so fast that she wouldn't be able to get off an emergency radio message. If she was being battered badly enough to break up, or the seas were so rough she could be capsized, the captain surely would have sent out a distress signal....Several ships of the* Marine Sulphur Queen's *class of ship had cracked and split. But no evidence was developed to explain how this ship, even if she had split in half, could go down so quickly as to leave no trace.*

Of the Coast Guard Board of Inquiry, Spencer concluded that "the little evidence that was presented only added to the mystery."

On August 1, 1974, six widows of merchants lost on the *Marine Sulphur Queen* were awarded $1.79 million in damages by a federal judge in New York. One month later, on September 1, 1974, Charles Berlitz published the

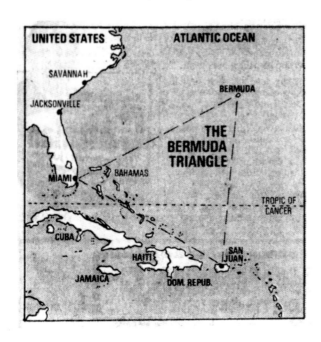

Map of the Bermuda Triangle (1974). *Courtesy of Detroit Free Press.*

worldwide bestseller *The Bermuda Triangle*. Berlitz's book includes an account of the disappearance of the *Marine Sulphur Queen* and a photo of the vessel, alongside those of the USS *Cyclops* and a TBM Avengers patrol similar to that of Flight 19. The *Marine Sulphur Queen* became part of Bermuda Triangle lore and began enjoying a claim to fame in paranormal circles.

The life jackets and debris recovered after the disappearance of the *Marine Sulphur Queen* were the first ever recovered from a ship or plane that vanished in the Bermuda Triangle.

WHEN THINGS WERE ALL said and done, twenty lawsuits regarding the disappearance of the *Marine Sulphur Queen* were settled out of court. Edith Martin was awarded $172,635[10] from the six-widow suit and left Austin for New York.

In early March 1963, Edith spoke with *Time* magazine. She had lingered so long at the wharf where the *Marine Sulphur Queen* disembarked because it was her husband's first voyage aboard the ship. Neither, of course, knew it would be his last. But Edith knew something. "I never wanted to be a seaman's wife," she said. "But he [Adam] had to earn a living. I came to see him off. The poor soul. I felt sorry for him when he first saw his new ship. It looked like an old garbage can afloat."

Edith passed away on April 23, 2001.

Did the *Marine Sulphur Queen* stop for repair or maintenance and then continue on, only to be destroyed by an explosion? Was the *Sulphur Queen* capsized by a towering wave or a freak sea? Or was the *Marine Sulphur Queen* swallowed by the Bermuda Triangle?

To this day, no one knows.

2
OF LIKE KIDNEY

I n the 1925 dime store classic book *Famous in the West*, Eugene Cunningham describes Billy the Kid and Jesse Evans as youngsters "of like kidney." The expression seems to have been fairly common in America in the mid- to late nineteenth century but was already old and approaching archaic in the years before the Great Depression. Sometimes expressions—like people—fade away slowly. And sometimes they disappear overnight.

In terms of Wild West outlaws, the legend of Billy the Kid—whose real name was Henry McCarty but was also known as William H. Bonney— often garners most of the headlines, pulp depictions and Hollywood film treatments. But the accounts rarely approach the truth. Unlike Emerson Hough's *Story of the Outlaw* (1907), they don't mention that the outlaw Jesse Evans didn't sweat Billy the Kid at all. "He [Evans] always said that the Kid might beat him with the Winchester," wrote Hough, "but that he feared no man living with the six-shooter." And, unlike *The Real Billy the Kid* (1936), by Miguel Antonio Otero—a former governor of New Mexico (when it was a territory)[11]—they don't mention that Evans's original relationship with the Kid was that of a mentor or that "Evans was so well known by the summer of 1877 that the Kid's outlaw image was heightened by his association with Jesse, not vice versa."[12] Or that Evans and the Kid—two men of like kidney—stayed in touch and crossed paths over and over again in sometimes brotherly and sometimes bloody interludes.

Not much of what is known about Jesse (sometimes spelled Jessie) Evans is confirmed or certain, but it is believed that he was born in Missouri or Texas in 1853 and might have been half Cherokee. Most accounts also suggest that Evans was a graduate of Washington and Lee College (in Virginia) and note that he was arrested along with his parents for counterfeiting in Elk City, Kansas, in 1871.

Evans arrived in New Mexico Territory in 1872 and is said to have met Billy the Kid in Silver City shortly thereafter. From there, he drifted and worked several ranches in the southeastern portion of the territory, eventually finding himself in the employ of legendary Texas cattle rancher John Chisum.[13] After he parted ways with Chisum, he became associated with the John Kinney Gang, which operated in Doña Ana County, New Mexico. The Kinney Gang stuck to acts of robbery and cattle rustling, and Kinney and Evans also proved to be of like kidney.

On December 31, 1875, Kinney, Evans and two other Kinney Gang members visited Las Cruces, New Mexico, for a night of revelry in a local saloon. They became embroiled in a disagreement with a group of U.S. cavalrymen from Fort Seldon and lost the ensuing brawl. Instead of heading home and leaving well enough alone, however, they opened fire on the saloon, and several people (including two U.S. cavalrymen and John Kinney) were killed or wounded.

Kinney subsequently laid low to recuperate, and Evans started the Jesse Evans Gang, which referred to itself as "The Boys." Kinney Gang regulars Billy Morton, Frank Baker, Jim McDaniels, Buffalo Bill Spawn, Dolly Graham, Tom Hill, Bob Martin, Nicholas Provencio and Manuel Segovia joined Evans.

When the Lincoln County War[14] started in 1878, Evans and the Kid were on opposing sides. Evans was part of the Lawrence Murphy/James Dolan/John Riley faction.[15] The Dolan contingent was allied with Lincoln County sheriff William Brady and aided by the Jesse Evans Gang. The Kid was part of the John Tunstall/Alexander McSween faction,[16] which organized its own posse of armed men, known as the Regulators, and had its own lawmen, including local constable Richard M. Brewer and deputy U.S. marshal Robert A. Widenmann. The two sides were vying for economic and political control of the community, and Evans and the Kid (and their associates) were simply hired guns; the ranchers, lawmen and politicians were the ones who issued the orders.

Fifteen warrants for Evans's arrest were issued between 1875 and 1878, and he was tried and acquitted for the killing of a Las Cruces man in 1877. Then, Evans was captured in the early spring of 1878, after the robbery of a rancher near Tularosa. He wound up being imprisoned at Fort Stanton while awaiting trial for charges related to the murder of John Tunstall but managed to post bail and flee. Later, Evans was present (and might have been an active participant) when New Mexico lawyer Huston Chapman was gunned down in cold blood at the behest of James Dolan. Chapman's murder led Evans to be arrested and re-imprisoned at Fort Stanton at the request of New Mexico Territory governor Lew Wallace.

Evans escaped his imprisonment at Fort Stanton on March 19, 1879, and fled to Texas. Evans and some of his gang apparently regrouped in West Texas and had a decent run as cattle rustlers around Fort Davis and Fort Stockton. But in late June 1880, a Texas Ranger contingent dispatched by legendary lawman Dan W. Roberts was sent out to the area to accost what Roberts referred to as a group of "robbers," assumed to be the last of the "'Billy the Kid' bunch."[17] The Rangers made short work of the new Evans group, tracking them quickly, cornering them like "blood hounds" (in the Chinati Mountains) and forcing them to surrender.

Evans was apprehended and placed in custody at Fort Davis. He managed to get a letter sent out, requesting help in orchestrating a jailbreak, but Fort Davis lawmen intercepted it. The details were conveyed in a report from Texas Ranger lieutenant C.L. Nevill to Texas Ranger general John B. Jones:

> *The prisoners are getting very restless. I have a letter they wrote to a friend of Evans in new Mexico calling himself Billy Antrim to cause their rescue, and to use his words he was "in a damned tight place only 14 rangers here at any time, ten on the scout and only four in camp right now," and that Antrim and a few men could take them out very easy. And if he could not do it now to meet him on the road to Huntsville as he was certain to go. I understand this man Antrim is a fugitive from somewhere and is a noted desperado. If he comes down and I expect he will, I will enlist him for a while and put him in the same mess with Evans and Co.*[18]

"Billy Antrim" was Billy the Kid,[19] and, though Evans and the Kid hadn't been on the same side of things for the last two and a half years or so, he still considered the Kid a man of like kidney, if not a friend.

The Kid never showed, and Evans attempted to escape at least once but was unsuccessful. He was tried and found guilty of the second-degree murder of Texas Ranger George Bingham in late 1880 and started his sentence at the Huntsville Penitentiary in Huntsville, Texas, on December 1 of that year. In mid-spring of 1882, Evans reportedly snuck away from a work detail and was never seen or heard from again.

Story of an Outlaw author Emerson Hough suggested that Evans eventually disappeared in Arizona Territory,[20] but there is little evidence or agreement about his fate. One thing, however, was abundantly clear. Outlaw life in the region was suddenly much less appealing. Billy the Kid had been gunned down by Pat Garrett on July 14, 1881, while Evans was in prison. Kinney had been arrested and convicted of cattle rustling in 1883, and when he was released in 1886, his former gang members and outlaw allies were all dead, imprisoned or in the wind.

Some believe Evans fled to Mexico. Others claim he became a civilian, one account suggesting he settled down in Fort Worth, married and raised six children. Historian Eve Ball[21] noted that a man claiming to be Jesse Evans's nephew told her that Jesse died paranoid on a large ranch in Texas in 1954. "He had not been out of the house in the daytime for 40 years," Ball wrote. "And even the closest neighbors did not know of his existence."

3
WITHOUT A TRACE

The first episode of the wildly popular *Dick Van Dyke Show* premiered on October 3, 1961. In the series debut, television comedy writer Rob Petrie (Dick Van Dyke) and his wife, Laura (Mary Tyler Moore), leave their sick son, Ritchie (Larry Mathews), with a babysitter and go to a party. After Rob and Laura arrive at the party, a nervous Laura phones the babysitter repeatedly to check on Ritchie, and Rob and Laura leave the party early to get home and be with their son. When they return home, Ritchie is fine.

Capitalizing on the trend of successful showbiz family sitcoms like *I Love Lucy*, which ended its original TV run only a few years earlier, *The Dick Van Dyke Show* introduced an idealized version of the American family—most American patriarchs were not TV comedy writers and fewer and fewer women were stay-at-home moms like Laura Petrie. By the 1960s, wives and mothers were entering the workforce in greater numbers. On Saturday, December 9, 1961, for example, the parents of eleven-year-old Wichita Falls boy Scott Andreas Sims (known as Andy) were both working. Andy's stepdad, William "Bill" Sims[22] (a National Guardsman when he wasn't an English instructor at Midwestern State University), had been called up for service at Fort Polk in Louisiana because the United States was navigating the Berlin Crisis.[23] Andy's mother, Ellen, was working a Saturday morning shift as a nurse.

The morning had been foggy, but by early afternoon, slivers of sunlight began piercing the clouds. Andy told his twelve-year-old brother, Donald,

Eleven-year-old Andy Sims disappeared in Wichita Falls on October 9, 1961. *Courtesy of Steven Douglass.*

that he was going outside to play. The Sims family lived in a corner lot at 4600 Stanford Avenue. It was located on the southwest side of the city in an unfinished suburban area that was still teased on every side by open prairie or pastureland. And Lake Wichita was a short walk away.

Ellen completed her shift at 1:00 p.m. and returned to the Sims residence at 2:30 p.m. Andy was reportedly gone, but Ellen wasn't concerned. In those days, it was common for kids to wander around and play all day, suffering only mild rebukes if they showed up home after dark. But by 8:00 p.m., Ellen became worried and contacted local authorities. Friends and family members conducted a search for Andy that night, but it was unsuccessful.

Andy went out to play and disappeared. He was never seen or heard from again.

THE POLICE FILES ON Andy Sims's missing persons case are now over six inches thick. For decades, the Wichita Falls Police Department received intermittent tips regarding Andy's disappearance, but none evolved into solid leads. In 2008, Charles Trainham,[24] who was a member of the department when Andy vanished, told the Associated Press that the investigation had been extremely difficult because "there was no crime scene" and "no tangible evidence." Despite this, former Wichita Falls police inspector Tony Fox, who was with the department from 1989 to 2014, believed the initial investigation "was very thorough." It involved the police department, the sheriff's department, the sheriff's mounted patrol, the marine corp reserves, a helicopter search unit from Shepherd Air Force Base and hundreds of volunteers. And later, the Texas Department of Public Safety and the FBI became involved.

After Andy was reported missing, one witness said a child matching Andy's description was seen at a Boy Scout hut near Lake Wichita at 3:00 p.m. The park was subsequently searched, and Lake Wichita was dragged, but neither effort yielded clues. Some of Andy's neighborhood friends said that Andy liked to explore some local caves near Fairway Boulevard, but the caves were examined and turned up nothing useful. Investigators also made fruitless visits to the homes of convicted sexual predators in the area.

Andy disappeared on his half-brother Steven Douglass's second birthday. Steven has been the driving force behind trying to find out what happened to Andy. *Courtesy of Steven Douglass.*

Sightings of Andy were later reported in Arkansas (where his grandparents lived), Missouri and Oklahoma, but none of these leads ever panned out.

At the time of his disappearance, Andy's birth father, Donald Ace Douglass, was living in California with his new wife and a young son, Steven Douglass. Donald Douglass was never a suspect in the investigation and called to check on the Wichita Falls Police Department's progress at regular intervals. He had received news of Andy's disappearance on Steven's second birthday.

Donald never spoke much about Andy to Steven, and as he grew older, Steven forgot about his missing half-brother. Steven didn't revisit the incident until he began researching his family history after his father passed away in 2001. By then, Steven had become a police officer in Ohio, and on the forty-seventh anniversary of Andy's disappearance, he visited Wichita Falls to do his own investigation. What he discovered was not reminiscent of an episode of *The Dick Van Dyke Show*. According to Steven Douglass, sources related to the investigation of Andy Sims's disappearance said that the primary suspect had always been a family member.

Bill and Ellen Sims moved to Austin in 1963 and went on to have two children of their own, David William Sims[25] and John Robert Sims. Bill and Ellen eventually divorced, however, and Bill remarried. Bill passed away in Austin on August 25, 2008, and Steven Douglass's investigation into his half-brother's disappearance led to newspaper coverage of the case later that year. Ellen didn't speak to reporters, and though it didn't uncover much new information, Steven's poking around led to her receiving a visit from Wichita Falls Police Department.

IN EARLY SEPTEMBER 2008, not long after Bill Sims's death, Steven Douglass requested a copy of the Wichita Falls Police Department file on Andy's disappearance. The city attorney responded by sending a letter to Texas's Attorney General Gregg Abbott on September 15, 2008, and forwarding a copy of the correspondence to Steven. The Office of the City Attorney's letter to Abbott is fairly straightforward, except it notes that the release of the requested police file "would interfere with the detection, investigation, or prosecution" of a possible criminal act that may have led to Andy's disappearance. This was after indicating the following: "The information sought is from a 1961 missing persons case. The WFPD Police Report itself is missing from City files, therefore, there is no front page, or basic, information to provide the requestor."

So, apparently, the city attorney decided to withhold a file that they had lost or weren't even in possession of.

Later, on November 8, 2013, Steven Douglass requested the case file on Andy's disappearance again, this time directly appealing to Attorney General Greg Abbott. The content of the letter is worth sharing here:

Dear Mr. Attorney General:

My name is Steve Douglass and I am 54 years old. On December 9, 1961, I celebrated my 2nd birthday with my parents and my two sisters at our home in Torrance, California. While I was blowing out the candles on my cake and ripping open presents, 1,300 miles away, in Wichita Falls, Texas, my 10 year old [sic] brother Andy was being murdered and his body being buried under a foundation or street under construction, where it has remained for the past 52 years. I never even knew he existed until 2001, when my father died and I was shown a newspaper article about Andy's "disappearance." I had seen the article before, as a young child, among the pictures and clippings my mother kept in a box in her closet, but I had no idea who this boy named Andy Sims was, or why my mother kept the article among other family mementos. You see, when his mother remarried, Andy and his older brother Donald took their stepfather's last name; until my mother showed me the article and explained it to me after my dad died, I was completely in the dark that this poor boy was my brother.

Even after the revelation of having not one, but two brothers I never knew, I still was under the impression that Andy had simply disappeared and no one ever knew what happened to him. However, this is not completely true. When I contacted the Wichita Falls Police Department, I found out there was much more to the story. Some of it I was told by retired officers and some came from old newspaper articles. Yet, the most amazing information was that while they could not prove anything, the police actually believed they knew what happened to my brother over 50 years ago. This hope of finally having closure was dashed when I was told that because it is still considered an "open case," I could not see the file on my brother's disappearance....As a retired police officer myself, I understand the reasoning behind the law. However, I am sure when it was established, no one ever expected to use it in a 52 year old [sic] case, that at the very best has the dust blown off the file once a year....I am writing this open letter to ask you to show some mercy to me as one of the victims of this horrible crime. I never knew my brother; he was brutally taken away from me on of all days, my birthday. Since I was told this horrendous story, I have not gone a day without thinking about, wondering about Andy. My stepbrother [Donald Sims] was so traumatized that he refuses to talk about Andy to this day. My father died not knowing what happened to his son. Hasn't our family suffered enough? I see that you and I are about the same age. How would you feel if it was your brother and you were denied any closure or peace of mind because those who are charged with helping you are afraid of unknown repercussions? I may even be able to help in the investigation. I have already given information to the detectives that they did not previously have. Please allow me to see the police file on my brother Andy. I will come to wherever you say, whenever you say. Please give me some peace. I beg you.

Attorney General Gregg Abbott's office acknowledged receipt of Douglass's letter on November 19, 2013, and responded on December 3, 2013. It stated that the Office of the Attorney General "had reviewed it's files" and that it had "no information responsive" to his request.

Steven Douglass entreated Attorney General Abbott's office to reconsider the decision in the matter, and the attorney general's office responded again on December 12, 2013. "Section 552.301 of the Public Information Act provides that a governmental body is prohibited from asking for a reconsideration of the attorney general's decision. Gov't Code 552.301(f). Although the governmental body has not asked us to reconsider the decision in this instance, we similarly decline your request to reconsider Open Records Letter No. 2008-15780."

In September 2020, Ellen Sims, then ninety years old, addressed Andy's disappearance. She said losing a child is not something you ever recover from. "Your life goes on and you have a life," she said. "But you don't really ever get over it." Ellen also said that she had to really fight the urge to be too overprotective of her other sons, David and William.

DID ANDY SIMS RUN away or simply vanish? Was Andy abducted and murdered? Was a family member involved in some way?

Without a body or a crime scene, the disappearance of Andy Sims might never be solved. But Steven Douglass revisits the tragedy every year—on his birthday.

4
GALVESTON GIRLS

Sondra Kay Ramber

On Wednesday, October 26, 1983, with Halloween just around the corner, a fourteen-year-old girl named Sondra Kay Ramber disappeared in Santa Fe, a small town on the mainland in Galveston County just north of the city of Galveston. Sondra's father, Alton Ladon Ramber, said that when he got home from work that afternoon, the front door was unlocked, and Sondra was missing. Mr. Ramber reported her disappearance the next day.

Local law enforcement personnel initially assumed Sondra was a runaway. Sondra's disappearance received little or no coverage in the contemporary local or regional newspapers, and she hasn't been seen or heard from since.

Michelle Doherty Thomas

On the evening of Saturday, October 5, 1985, seventeen-year-old Michelle Doherty Thomas left her parents' home with friends to meet some more friends at the now-demolished Cave Club on Stewart Beach in Galveston. The following day was her son's first birthday, but she didn't make the party. Michelle was never seen or heard from again.

Michelle had started using drugs in high school and married at the age of sixteen. She got pregnant soon after, but she and her husband got into some trouble, and the marriage didn't work out.

Michelle Doherty Thomas disappeared in Galveston on October 5, 1985. *Courtesy of Galveston Daily News.*

The trouble Michelle and her husband got into involved burglary charges, and local law enforcement officers parleyed Michelle and her husband's fear of hard time into the two becoming informants in a narcotics case. Michelle and her husband separated in the spring of 1985, and Michelle committed herself to raising her son. She began working at a gas station that her family ran in Galveston, but she started hearing rumors. There was talk in some circles that hinted that the party or parties affected by Michelle's stint as an informant might be planning to retaliate.

On the night of her disappearance, Michelle had been picked up from her parents' house by two male friends, twenty-one-year-old Carlos Garcia Jr. and twenty-year-old Warren Lyn Richardson (who was driving). After Michelle was reported missing, Garcia and Richardson told the Galveston County Sheriff's Department that when they stopped at a convenience store, Michelle got into another car with two other men. And they insisted she did so voluntarily.

A month after Michelle's disappearance, a source told authorities that Michelle had been murdered because she "wore a wire" and served as an informant. The source also indicated that her remains could be found in a large field near the Alta Loma neighborhood of Santa Fe.

When Garcia and Richardson were indicted for kidnapping Michelle in December 1985, they changed their stories. They claimed that everything was fine until they stopped at an intersection on FM 517 west of Dickinson (northeast of Santa Fe). They said two men jumped out of another car and forcibly removed Michelle from Richardson's vehicle. Michelle's purse and jacket had been left behind, and Richardson told police he disposed of them.

In February 1986, twenty-one-year-old Tony Locke of Alta Loma was indicted for capital murder in connection with Michelle's disappearance, and Garcia and Richardson were accused of "terrorizing" her and delivering her to Locke.

The charges against Garcia and Richardson were subsequently dropped, and eventually, the indictment of Locke was shelved. The prosecution had no body and no murder weapon, and there was no scientific evidence linking Locke to Michelle's death.

MICHELLE DOHERTY THOMAS MADE some mistakes when she was young and got in with a questionable crowd. The Santa Fe community and the surrounding area was dealing with serious drug problems at the time, and local law enforcement personnel used a possible burglary charge to coerce Michelle—a teenage soon-to-be single mother—into helping them make some headway in the local "war" on drugs.

These machinations apparently led to Michelle's disappearance.

SHELLEY KATHLEEN SIKES

It was Memorial Day weekend in 1986. Galveston Island was packed with tourists, and Shelley Kathleen Sikes had a great job at the popular upscale Gaido's Seafood Restaurant, located at the 3800th block of Seawall Boulevard. The nineteen-year-old, who was voted Miss School Spirit, Most Talented and Best Personality at Texas City High before she left for the University of Texas at Austin, was excited to be back home. She was happy to be closer to her family and her boyfriend, Mark Spurgeon.

Toward the end of her evening shift on May 24, Shelley phoned Mark and told him she planned to stop by. When Shelley didn't show up, Spurgeon called Gaido's. A waiter told him Shelley had left just after 11:30 p.m. Mark jumped in his car and went looking for her. By 12:45 a.m., Mark was worried and reached out to his father, Jim Spurgeon. They drove to Galveston and then drove back up I-45 North, the route Shelley usually took home. They spotted Shelley's blue 1980 Ford Pinto off a northbound feeder road on I-45. The driver's side window had been smashed, and blood was everywhere, but Shelley was missing.

Mark and Jim Spurgeon drove to the Texas City Police Station and requested assistance. It was not the city police department's most flattering moment.

"There was one guy in there," Mark later testified. "I explained the situation—that she [Shelley] was overdue, we found the car, the window was shattered, and blood was all over. I asked if they would help and he [the officer] didn't say anything. He just stood there looking at me."

When a second officer appeared, Mark repeated the details and asked the officers for assistance in contacting local hospitals. Mark said that the second officer's response was less than reassuring. "Well, I guess so," the officer replied. The Spurgeons became frustrated and left. They began contacting hospitals on their own.

The hospitals reported no recent patients matching Shelley's description, so the Spurgeons contacted the Galveston County Sheriff's Department, and a deputy agreed to meet them at Shelley's car. While Deputy Sheriff Larry Powers questioned Mark, Mr. Spurgeon re-examined the sandy area in front of Shelley's Pinto. He found two footprints, one from a bare left foot and one from a right shoe, which apparently belonged to Shelley. Deputy Powers discovered Shelley's left shoe in the floor of the car beneath the steering wheel. The key was still in the ignition, the driver's side window was smashed in instead of out and there was, as previously noted, a significant amount of blood. It was spattered on the steering wheel, the driver's side door and a gym bag in the passenger seat. Splattered mud outside the car indicated that the Pinto's wheels had spun in an attempt to free the vehicle.

Though the Spurgeons urged the responding deputy to report the Pinto and its missing driver as a crime scene, the officer called it in as the scene of an accident. Two wreckers showed up and a passing driver stopped, all touching the car and contaminating what would eventually be viewed as a crime scene. Several of Shelley's belongings were found in the car, including the gym bag and a Gaido's apron that held fifty-three dollars in cash. Everything was handed over to Mark Spurgeon rather than being kept as evidence.

The Spurgeons notified the Sikes family after they left the scene, and the Sikes family waited the customary twenty-four hours and filed a missing person report. By Tuesday, the incident was being characterized as a possible kidnapping or homicide. Drivers reported seeing Shelley's Pinto being forced off the road and a White man forcibly removing Shelley from her vehicle and placing her in his truck. When one passerby stopped to inquire if everything was okay, the White man told them it was a "family matter." Witnesses also described the truck taking off rapidly and erratically northbound on Interstate 45. Officers from the Galveston County Organized Crime Control Unit (OCCU) and the Sheriff's Department believed Shelley was forced off the road and an assailant punched in her window to get to her after she locked her doors.

Shelley Kathleen Sikes disappeared in Galveston on December 24, 1986. *Courtesy of* Galveston Daily News.

Over the next several months, family members, concerned citizens and local businesses offered rewards, posted flyers, paid for billboard notices and printed T-shirts to aid in the search for Shelley, but nothing turned up. On November 12, 1986, a clerk at a Marshall, Texas convenience store saw a girl he thought looked like Shelley based on a poster he had seen in the local post office. The girl was accompanied by a man, but the clerk hadn't gotten the license plate number of the vehicle they were traveling in, and local authorities were unsuccessful in determining their whereabouts.

THIRTEEN MONTHS AFTER SHELLEY'S disappearance, a twenty-nine-year-old construction worker named John Robert King saw a "missing girl" poster with Shelley's face on it in Ciudad Juarez (Mexico) and attempted suicide in an El Paso motel. A former Bacliff (north central Galveston County) resident, King had relocated to the El Paso area to avoid the memories of what he had done to Shelley Sikes as the one-year anniversary of the incident approached. The anniversary caught up with him anyway.

King wrote two suicide notes, admitting that he and another man, thirty-two-year-old Seabrook resident Gerald Peter Zwarst, a pipefitter, had abducted Shelley. The notes also included apologies to his parents for causing them so much pain. King tried to hang himself by his bootlaces and slit his wrists, but both suicide attempts were unsuccessful. Confronted by his incompetence and his guilt, he contacted the El Paso Police Department and confessed. They picked him up on June 22 and transferred him to Galveston.

On Thursday, June 25, 1987, King and Zwarst were both arrested and charged with aggravated kidnapping and held on $100,000 bonds. King said he and Zwarst had been partying and smoking PCP-laced marijuana at East Beach on Galveston Island on May 24, 1986, and that they encountered Shelley heading out of Broadway Avenue (which turns into Interstate 45) that night. King said he and Zwarst followed her across the Galveston Causeway in Zwarst's truck, and Zwarst forced her off the road. The pair then stuffed a "groggy" Shelley in the floorboard of the truck and drove her around the mainland. King remembered Zwarst asking him if he was going to rape Shelley, but King claimed all he did was take her to the bed of the truck and lay on top of her. Both men admitted to burying Shelley at a secluded spot on Gordy Street in Bacliff, but neither would admit to killing her. King couldn't remember if Shelley was dead or alive, and at one point, he described the dirt over her moving after they buried her.

King said they took a shovel and started beating the earth where they saw movement until it stopped. Zwarst admitted to selling the truck they used to abduct Shelley, and the FBI located it in South Carolina shortly after. Both men gave investigators detailed information that only the perpetrators of Shelley's abduction could have known.

King agreed to lead investigators to Shelley's body if they first let him visit his father, who actually lived on Gordy Street. After King's one-and-a-half-hour visit with his father, however, he said he couldn't remember where Shelley was buried.

Since investigators were unable to produce Shelley's body, King and Zwarst were indicted and prosecuted separately for the strongest charge the authorities could bring, aggravated kidnapping. They were convicted in 1988 and sentenced to life in prison. Both men were offered plea deals in exchange for the location of Sikes's remains, but neither cooperated. Zwarst later reconsidered and offered to lead lawmen to Shelley's body, but his directions proved inaccurate.

John Robert King died in prison in October 2015.

Zwarst was first up for parole in 2007 and has petitioned the parole board every five years since. Members of the Sikes family attend every parole hearing. In 2012, Sikes's sister, Dana Wild, lamented the process. "Even if he gets denied parole this time and gets put up for five more years," Wild said, "I know that in five more years we're going to be doing this again. Every time that the sore begins to heal, then something scratches the surface off, and it's bleeding all over again."

On Saturday, May 25, 1996—ten years after Shelley's disappearance—her family placed a headstone for her and held a funeral service at the Galveston Memorial Park Cemetery in Hitchcock (just northwest of Galveston on the mainland). Shelley's father, Eddie Sikes, said, "Hardly a day goes by I don't think of her" and noted that the plot and the headstone will give his daughter's loved ones a place to remember her. Mr. Sikes said they just wanted to celebrate Shelley's life and that the grave would be a place where they could feel "close to her."

Zwarst is up for parole again in 2022.

Suzanne Rene Richerson

Suzanne Rene Richerson was on the cusp of exciting things. In the fall of 1988, she was in the middle of completing the first semester of her senior year at Texas A&M University–Galveston. The twenty-two-year-old's goal was to complete her bachelor's degree and then pursue a degree in maritime law. She was taking a full course load and working as a night clerk at the upscale Casa Del Mar Condominiums-Hotel (at 6102 Seawall Boulevard in Galveston) to pay the bills. Everything was going according to plan until the morning of October 7, 1988.

When a Casa Del Mar security guard's rounds took him past the front desk at 6:00 a.m., Rene was fine. She only had one hour left on her shift. But when the daytime clerk came on duty at 6:50 a.m., Rene was nowhere to be found. Her textbooks, purse, wallet and car keys were still at the reception desk.

A quick search revealed that no money was taken from the reception desk cash register, but there were scuff marks behind the counter. And a brown leather shoe thought to belong to Rene was found in the parking lot. The Galveston Police Department was contacted, and officers soon arrived to investigate, but aside from the shoe, which had no useful fingerprints, the crime scene offered no actionable clues. It appeared that Rene had been dragged away from the reception desk, presumably losing her shoe as she fought and kicked at her assailant or assailants in the parking lot. But there was no way to be sure.

The 750-student enrollment at Texas A&M University–Galveston was stunned. It was like a small town where everybody knew each other. Rene's friends were distraught, and some of her professors were devastated. The university's vice president of student services considered Rene a friend and called her a "bright, talented, had-everything-going-for-her type of kid."

By October 21, 1988, Rene's classmates at Texas A&M University–Galveston were holding vigils and had posted thousands of flyers all over Seawall Boulevard and Galveston and beyond. "You can't drive anywhere between here and Houston without seeing her picture in store windows," Rene's mother, Kathy, said. But Mrs. Richerson was scared. She and Rene's father, Clyde, begged anyone who might have witnessed the abduction to come forward.

Excepting four psychics—who provided nothing useful—no one did.

Local law enforcement personnel got nowhere, so the Richersons hired a private detective named Willie Payne. An anonymous tip led Payne to a site in Brazoria County, but when he examined it with local lawmen and search dogs, they found nothing.

In December 1988, an anonymous caller made repeated calls to authorities to discuss Rene Richerson's disappearance. The individual claimed he took part in Rene's abduction, murder and burial. In some conversations he wept. In one communication, the anonymous suspect indicated that the names of the other two kidnappers were Johnny and Barry, and he claimed they buried Richerson's body fifteen to twenty miles west of Hitchcock. The individual also said that Johnny and Barry were pipeline workers and that Rene was interred on top of a stretch of pipeline.

The new information generated no productive leads. Searches of the area again proved fruitless.

In late August 1989, the Richersons appeared on Bill Meshel's *Galveston Night Talk* on KGBC AM radio with Eddie Sikes. All of the parents wanted to continue getting the word out about their missing daughters, and the Richersons, in particular, were frustrated. During the course of the live discussion, Mr. Richerson revealed that the Galveston Police Department had not checked all of the rooms in the Casa Del Mar Condominiums-Hotel or interviewed all of the lodgers at the Casa Del Mar the night of Rene's disappearance.

On October 29, 1989, a group of fishermen discovered a human skull on the Highland Bayou, northwest of Hitchcock on the mainland. Local investigators thought it might be part of Rene Richerson's remains, but they were mistaken. In December 1989, Payne had a team dig up a portion of the backyard of a La Marque residence in Brazoria County, but this effort also proved futile.

Payne was still working the case in October 1991, but he was frustrated. "We know who killed her," Payne said. "The police know who killed her. Her parents know who killed her. It just can't be proven."

In December 1998, the Galveston Police Department returned to Brazoria County after another anonymous tip hinting at the location of Rene Richerson's remains. Investigators produced almost three dozen bone fragments from Cloud Bayou, near the Galveston County line—but none belonged to Rene Richerson.

5
THIN AIR

In every missing person's case, there is invariably some level of sadness—even for people who never knew the missing man, woman or child. There are also questions.

Were they abducted?

Were they tortured or sexually assaulted?

Were they murdered and dumped somewhere, or did they just simply sneak away to start another life?

Is it possible they're still alive?

In most incidents discussed in this volume, relatives, friends and colleagues of the missing person (or persons) were contacted for comment at the time, and it was not uncommon for them to be involved in appeals to potential captors in hopes of the victim's safe and speedy return. The people connected to the missing person were, after all, victims themselves, and each, in their own way, experienced some sense of emptiness or regret regarding the disappearances. They answered questions from investigators (and reporters) and participated in searches. They posted rewards, held vigils, put up flyers and met with psychics. They hoped against hope.

One case, however, conspicuously deviates from this pattern.

ON MONDAY, DECEMBER 18, 1978, a small, Beechcraft Baron twin-engine plane was found in a long-unused hangar located at Loop 197 and Smith Road in Texas City. The aircraft's serial number had been obscured, four of the seats in the six-seat aircraft had been removed (and stacked in the back) and the carpet had been "ripped away."[26] There were also blood stains inside the craft and a bullet hole in the roof of the cockpit.

On Tuesday, December 19, investigators found several discarded flight bags and twenty empty five-gallon containers two and a half miles from the hangar, beneath some trees at the 8100th block of FM 1764. Police Sergeant Deril Oliver, who spent most of the day dusting the plane for fingerprints, told reporters that they had received "no word from the pilot." Police captain Savas Saragoza said that a local resident had spotted the aircraft in the hangar and that "traces of what appeared to be marijuana" were found at the site. Saragoza also announced that the Texas City Police Department would be working on the case with the FBI.

The twin-engine plane belonged to Seaback Aviation in Tomball and was used for charter flights. The missing pilot's name was Milton Wayne Sims (although some newspapers referred to him as Melton Sims). The charter plane had been booked by a "Michael Jackson" for a return flight to Houston Intercontinental Airport on Saturday, December 16. Sims, twenty-eight, had flown "Jackson"—who paid $400 roundtrip—to Huntsville from Houston the night before and then returned to Tomball.

FBI agent Nick O'Hara said air traffic controllers lost radio contact with Sims on Saturday morning, and investigators believe the plane was hijacked after it took off. Witnesses reported that the plane was spotted landing, taxiing and refueling and then taking off immediately in Teague (eighty miles northeast of Huntsville) and then Rockport (290 miles south of Teague on the Gulf Coast). When the airport manager in Teague was shown photographs of Sims, she claimed that he was not piloting the plane when it rushed through.

Larry Leffingwell, the president of Seaback Aviation, felt sure the incident was drug related and stated that Sims was extremely reliable. "The plane was parked in a hangar and the identification number on the exterior had been spray-painted over with white paint," Leffingwell said. "Sims would fight like a buzzsaw. He would never go along with this type of deal."

"It appears he [Sims] was taken hostage," said Texas City police chief Renkin DeWalt. "The pilot [Sims] was outstanding and we have no reason to believe he was involved." DeWalt also offered that "Sims apparently was shot before the plane was flown to the Texas City airport." And investigators noted that the gas tanks of the aircraft contained "140 gallons of fuel, enough to fly over 1,000 miles nonstop."

The address "Michael Jackson" supplied to book the charter turned out to be phony.

On Saturday December 22, 1978, Seaback Aviation offered a $20,000 reward for information on Sims's disappearance, and that was pretty much the end of the story. The day before, the *Longview News-Journal* had reported that Sims was described by friends as a good pilot and a quiet bachelor, but no friends or family were named.

One year later, a rice farmer in Alvin, Texas, found a skeleton in a rice field with a bullet hole in the skull. Local authorities opined that it might be Milton Sims, but an FBI spokesman was quick to undermine the suggestion. He mentioned that "new information had been received" that suggested the remains found in the field were not those of the missing pilot.

Milton Sims disappeared into thin air on December 17, 1978. *Courtesy of the Texas Missing Person Directory.*

Milton Sims vanished into thin air. And then the investigation into his disappearance vanished, and his name fell completely out of the headlines.

TO BE FAIR, MILTON Sims's disappearance was a jurisdictional nightmare. Yes, the FBI handled the case as a whole, but it must have been unclear who besides Texas City could help. Law enforcement personnel in Huntsville? Teague? Rockport?

In terms of Sims's abduction and/or murder, investigators had no body, no murder weapon and could not establish definitively where the abduction or murder had even taken place. All they had was a suspected motive. After the skeleton was found in Alvin, an FBI spokesman discussed what might have happened to Sims. "Our inclination is that the incident has a drug-related background," he said. "Any time a plane's seats are removed it can be assumed that they were removed for cargo. What that cargo might be is up for speculation, but you can make your own guess."

From 1978 to 1979, law enforcement agencies seized over $250 million[27] in marijuana that drug traffickers smuggled into the United States via the Texas coastline—and authorities estimated that this was only a fraction of what actually entered the country along that route. The drug smugglers used cargo ships, fishing boats, sailboats and small aircraft. In fact, Customs Service agents confiscated twenty tons of marijuana (with an estimated value of $12 million) from a shrimping boat named the *Agnes Pauline*[28] in Port Arthur less than three weeks before the twin-engine plane Sims piloted was discovered gassed up and ready to go in a Texas City hangar. And one year later—actually during the same week local law enforcement theorized that the skeleton discovered in Alvin might be Sims—authorities seized one hundred thousand pounds of marijuana as it was being unloaded from a ship at the Intracoastal Marina in Freeport.

Did Milton Sims fall through the cracks of the ongoing drug trafficking investigations at the local and regional levels at the time? Was Sims's murderer offered a deal in exchange for testimony implicating bigger fish in the local drug trade? Or was he just collateral damage in a drug war that still persists today?

We might never know.

6
LOST FATHERS

The Gothic Revival–style Immaculate Conception Cathedral in Brownsville is a Texas marvel. At a glance, the facility is impressive and an undeniably stunning monument to the Catholic faith and the miracle it's named for. But the structure and all of its adornments are not the only incredible aspects of the cathedral. It also has an extraordinary backstory that is punctuated by two disappearances.

Dedicated the Immaculate Conception Church in July 1856, its structure is still composed of 250,000 of the original bricks, retains twenty-nine original stained-glass windows (depicting dramatic scenes from the Bible) and still has the original wooden pews, which comfortably seat almost four hundred. Its magnificent chandeliers, which hang down from the vaulted nave ceilings, were shipped from France in 1865. Originally candle-lit, they were retrofitted with light sockets (when Brownsville received electrical service in the early twenteith century) and only the crystal in them has been replaced since. The Stations of the Cross were placed on the cathedral walls in 1907, the tabernacle and the bishop's chair date to the 1800s and the antique pipe organ arrived in 1935.

In 1849, the Missionary Oblates of Mary Immaculate became the first Catholic priests to celebrate Mass in the Brownsville area. A parish was established, and a small frame chapel was built, but there was no central or official mission, so the Oblates' presence was gone within two years.

A small contingent of Oblates of Mary Immaculate returned in 1852 under the direction of Father Superior Jean Maurice Casimir Verdet. Born in Malaucène, France, on September 22, 1825, Verdet studied theology at the main seminary in Avignon and was ordained to the priesthood on September 23, 1848. Verdet deemed the original small frame chapel in Brownsville inadequate and petitioned his superiors for permission to build a larger, permanent place of worship. His request was approved.

In 1853, Father Pierre Yves Keralum, a former carpenter and building tradesman, was transferred from the first college-level Catholic seminary in Galveston to Brownsville to assist Father Verdet in the new church's construction. Keralum was born in Quimper, France, on March 2, 1817. He began his theological studies at the Notre-Dame de l'Osler in October 1851 and completed them at the main seminary in Marseilles in 1852. He was ordained to the priesthood on February 15, 1852.

The foundation of the structure for the Immaculate Conception Church was laid in 1854. In August 1856, Father Verdet undertook a sea voyage from Brownsville to New Orleans aboard a U.S. Mail paddlewheel steamship called the *Nautilus*, intent on securing further funding for the project and purchasing timber for the construction effort. After a stop in Galveston, the *Nautilus* encountered a violent gale in the Gulf of Mexico: "A significant maritime tragedy of the era occurred off the Texas coast on August 8, 1856, when the steamship *Nautilus*, bound from Galveston to New Orleans carrying thirty thousand dollars in specie, thirty passengers, one hundred horses, and forty head of cattle, was pounded mercilessly by a hurricane. The *Nautilus* was wrecked, and its wreckage was scattered along the coast from Sabine pass to Point Bolivar; reports at the time noted all hands were lost except a lone black man who clung to a cotton bale."[29]

Though the death of Father Verdet was a terrible tragedy and regarded by Oblates Bishop Eugène de Mazenod (canonized a saint by Pope John Paul II on December 3, 1995) as an "irremediable" loss, Father Keralum was subsequently entrusted with the church's completion. Father Keralum modified the plans for the new church and saw the project through to completion. He supervised the baking of the bricks, designed the pulpit and altar, fashioned the pilasters and chose the materials for the floor and the roof of the structure.

As the topside covering of the stone-foundation church was wooden, Father Keralum was concerned about its weight-bearing capacity and got creative. He crafted the nave ceiling of sky-blue canvas, lending it a dynamic, ethereal effect that has been restored and maintained to its original splendor to the present day.

Father Keralum also oversaw the construction of the priests' housing, the nuns' convent and the rectory building. The church's eighty-three-foot bell tower was completed in 1863, and over most of the next decade, Father

Father Keralum was part of the Cavalry of Christ, a group of Oblate missionaries who traveled on horseback to remote ranches and villages in the Rio Grande Valley. *Courtesy of Catholic Advance (1912).*

Keralum also helped with numerous Catholic construction projects in the Rio Grande Valley, including the San Augustin Cathedral in Laredo.

Besides his work on Catholic buildings in the region, Father Keralum was also one of the early members of the Cavalry of Christ. The Cavalry of Christ were priests who traveled long distances on horseback to minister to Catholics living in isolated reaches of the Rio Grande Valley. On November 9, 1872, though in his fifties and nearly blind, Keralum began a missionary circuit to visit the 70 to 120 villages and ranches he considered part of his parish. On November 12, 1872, Keralum left the Cano Ranch (in Hidalgo County) and, like Father Verdet, disappeared.

A few days later, his horse—minus its saddle—was discovered grazing in the area. Foul play was suspected, but investigations proved fruitless.

IN 1874, THE VICARIATE apostolic of Brownsville was established, and the Immaculate Conception Church became a cathedral.

Ten years after Father Keralum's disappearance, his remains were discovered undisturbed by a couple of cowhands near Mercedes and returned to the Immaculate Conception Cathedral. Father Keralum was rescued from oblivion, but Father Verdet was not.

In the decades that followed, the Immaculate Conception rectory would repeatedly serve as a haven for priests who fled revolutions in Mexico, and in 1980, the Immaculate Conception complex was listed in the National Register of Historic Places.

7
VIRGINIA CARPENTER

In some missing person cases the public or the press lose interest, and the victim fades into oblivion. In some cases—Milton Sims, for instance—law enforcement agencies seem to lose interest or hit a dead end, and a missing person investigation is consigned to oblivion. Public interest also often wanes when the aggrieved families or loved ones relocate or don't spend a lot of time pursuing the case themselves. Ellen Sims (no relation to Milton) wasn't terribly keen on discussing her son Andy's disappearance in 1961 and has never participated in retrospective newspaper coverage of her missing boy's fate. The parents of all of the aforementioned missing Galveston girls, save Sondra Kay Ramber's father, refused to let go and actually compelled law enforcement personnel to pursue leads years after their daughters had gone missing. That meant their cases stayed in the public eye. Hazel Carpenter remained involved in the investigation into the disappearance of her daughter for decades.

Hazel's only child, Mary Virginia Carpenter, started her college studies at Texarkana Junior College and continued at Texas State Teachers College for Women (now known as Texas Women's University) in Denton from September 1945 to February 1946. Then, Hazel grew ill, and Virginia came home to help take care of her. Virginia started working at the Holman-Kitrell Insurance Agency of Texarkana and continued her studies part-time at Texarkana Junior College. In the spring of 1948, Virginia decided to continue her studies at Texas State Teachers College for Women.

On Tuesday, June 1, 1948, Virginia Carpenter left Texarkana on the westbound Texas and Pacific Railway train (Texas Special no. 31) headed for Denton. She was dressed in a light white chambray dress with green, red and brown stripes; red shoes; and a small white straw hat with a white feather. She was also wearing a Wittnauer gold wristwatch and carrying a red purse with fifteen to twenty dollars in it. On the train, she met Marjorie Webster, a middle-aged schoolteacher who was also from Texarkana and headed to the Texas State Teachers College for Women to enroll in summer courses. When they arrived in Denton at approximately 9:00 p.m., they shared a taxi to the Brackenridge Dormitory. But when they got to the campus, Virginia realized she'd forgotten the trunk she checked before boarding the train. Webster said she would accompany Virginia back to the train station, but their taxi driver, Edgar Ray Zachary, seemed amicable, and Virginia told Webster that she'd be fine.

Virginia's friendly, trusting nature probably led to her untimely demise.

The next morning, Virginia's trunk was discovered "thrown in a careless manner" on the lawn in front of Brackenridge Dorm. As Virginia never checked in at the dorm, no one initially knew who the trunk belonged to, and it was simply moved inside. A few days later, Virginia's former boyfriend Kenny Branham tried to reach her at the dorm and discovered that she had never checked in. He contacted Hazel Carpenter immediately, and she contacted the Denton police. Hazel traveled to Denton on June 5 and remained there until June 18.

Virginia Carpenter disappeared at what is now Texas Women's University in Denton on June 1, 1948. *Courtesy of* Waco News-Tribune.

In the next few days and weeks, the investigation conducted by the Denton police centered on Virginia and Marjorie Webster's amicable taxi driver, Edgar Ray Zachary. He admitted freely and repeatedly that he was the last one to see Virginia Carpenter. And his story never varied. He said he and Virginia returned to the train station but were informed they would have to come back for her trunk the following morning. Zachary swore he told Virginia that if she signed the back of the claim ticket, he would pick up the trunk the next morning and drop it off at the dorm himself. Then, he swore he drove her back to the Brackenridge Dorm, where, according to Zachary, she stepped out of the taxi and immediately started talking to two young men she recognized in a cream-colored convertible. Zachary said he heard her ask them "Well, what are you doing here?" Zachary then allegedly placed her belongings—including a black pasteboard hatbox, a brown suitcase and a matching makeup case on the curb—and drove away.

In short order, Zachary was the prime suspect, but authorities did search for the cream-colored convertible and question Virginia's former boyfriend, Branham. The police never located a cream-colored convertible in the area, much less on the campus that evening, and Branham's alibi checked out.[30] Then, a bus agent in DeQueen, Arkansas, reported seeing Virginia there on Saturday, June 12. Authorities investigated the sighting and determined that the bus agent had been mistaken. By mid-July, after Zachary had been interviewed dozens of times, he took and passed a lie detector test, and investigators found themselves at a dead end.

In December 1948, Hazel Carpenter was still hopeful but realistic. "I must find her," Mrs. Carpenter said, "even though I do have to accept [it might be] just her lifeless form. I have accepted death in the past, and I can again, and would prefer that to some of the things that could have happened to her." Denton police chief Jack Shepherd said he did not think Virginia was dead. "I don't have any evidence that violence occurred," he said. "Nor do I have any of course, that violence did not occur. We don't know why the girl disappeared. We've checked out a lot of rumors. Nothing has come of any of them."

By January 1949, a nationwide search for Virginia Carpenter involving the FBI, the Texas Rangers and the Skip-Tracer Company of New York[31] was underway. Theories about Virginia's whereabouts ranged from her experiencing amnesia after a possible blow to the head, her being forced into "White slavery"[32] or her body being weighted down with rocks and lying at the bottom of Lake Dallas (which was only ten miles away). By the one-year anniversary of Virginia's disappearance, Hazel had moved to Dallas to be closer to Denton (and the investigation) and was working at the East Dallas Baptist Church.

In August 1949, Zachary was still the chief suspect, and the Denton County Sheriff's Department obtained a warrant and dug up portions of his backyard. The excavation yielded a hacksaw blade, two small bones and some buttons. The bones turned out to be canine, and Hazel Carpenter didn't recognize any of the buttons. The rumors and clues surrounding Virginia's disappearance dried up, and the case went cold.

THERE MIGHT NEVER HAVE been another development or clue in the Virginia Carpenter case if Edgar Ray Zachary hadn't made headlines again—and not because the former Denton taxi driver had won an all-expense-paid vacation to Monaco compliments of the new, wildly popular *The Price Is Right* gameshow.[33] Zachary made the headlines again because he was accused of attacking another young woman.

On Friday, August 16, 1957, a twenty-five-year-old Grand Prairie mother of three and employee of Chance Vaught Aircraft Company showed up at the Farmer's Branch Police Station on the verge of hysterics. She said that Zachary, a longtime acquaintance, asked her to meet him at the Dallas Sportatorium[34] to discuss a business opportunity. When the young woman arrived at 8:00 p.m., Zachary was waiting in another car. She said Zachary asked her to drive him in her car to see a man south of Dallas. The woman and Zachary drove to Wilmer, headed east on Belt Line Road and turned on a gravel drive near the Trinity River bridge. Zachary pointed at a house and noted there was no car in the driveway. He said that his friend didn't appear to be there.

When the woman turned around in the empty driveway and started back down the gravel road, Zachary pulled a gun on her and demanded that she have sex with him. The woman resisted, and Zachary struck her twice in the head with the gun. The woman never lost consciousness and continued to struggle. Zachary's attempt to sexually assault her was "unsuccessful," so he tied her hands and feet, gagged her and forced her into the front seat floorboard of her car.

As Zachary drove back toward Dallas, he started crying and implored the woman to forgive him, requesting that if she reported the incident, that she didn't do so in Dallas. When Zachary and the woman got back to the Sportatorium, he released her, and she went straight to her brother's house. After conferring with her brother, she drove to the Farmers Branch Police Station[35] and filed a complaint.

When Dallas County sheriff Bill Decker put out wanted bulletins for Zachary on charges of attempted rape, the authorities in Denton got wind of it. On Tuesday, August 20, 1957, Zachary—now forty-nine, balding and heavyset but amicable as ever—appeared at the Dallas County Sheriff's Department with his lawyer, Hal Jackson, of Denton. He admitted to meeting the young woman at the Sportatorium, but submitted a written denial of the attempted sexual assault charges against him. In fact, he tried to play the victim himself. He portrayed himself as a put-upon married man with four daughters and a son and complained that his wife was currently suing him for divorce. Then, Denton County sheriff Wiley Barnes and deputy Jack Shepherd—who had been the chief of police in Denton when Virginia Carpenter disappeared—arrived to question Zachary about the older case. When reporters tracked down Hazel Carpenter, who had remarried and was living in Amarillo, she spoke frankly. "I've felt she was dead from the beginning," Hazel admitted. "But I've always tried not to let that feeling keep me from tracking down every possible lead." She said she had received tips about her daughter's whereabouts from New York to California and that a Fort Worth man had even tried to blackmail her, claiming that Virginia would be returned if she paid him $500.

Zachary eventually agreed to take a second lie detector test but only regarding Virginia Carpenter's disappearance—not the new charges.

On August 26, 1957, Zachary's second lie detector test regarding the fate of Virginia Carpenter revealed definite "variations and reactions." Worse still, when reporters located and spoke with Zachary's estranged wife, who was then living in Midland, she torpedoed a key aspect of his original alibi. She claimed that he had actually returned home around 2:00 or 3:00 a.m. on June 2, 1948—not 10:00 p.m. on June 1, as he had stated.

On August 28, 1957, Zachary was charged with attempted rape, and his bail was set at $25,000.[36] On September 6, a second judge reduced Zachary's bond to $16,000.[37] On September 24, Zachary's trial was postponed when his defense attorneys asked for a sanity hearing. The sitting judge excused the jury panel called for the case and granted a postponement for a complete psychiatric examination.

On November 1, 1957, Zachary was released from the Dallas County jail on a $5,000 bond after the twenty-five-year-old woman who filed the complaint that led to the sexual assault charges against him decided she would not testify against him in court. Hal Jackson subsequently posted Zachary's bond and dropped his request for a sanity hearing.

In February 1959, Willie Philpott, a Black man who was a suspect in a number of murders in North Texas, was looked at and then cleared as a suspect in the disappearances of Virginia Carpenter and Euclid T. Fant, a Sherman man who disappeared in 1958. After that, the case grew ice cold and remained so for almost forty years.

In 1998, an elderly informant told a retired Denton police officer and Denton County sheriff's deputy that Virginia had been raped and murdered by two men and buried beneath a stock tank dam a few miles east of the campus of Texas Women's University. The retired officer relayed the information to Denton County sheriff Weldon Lucas, and the department spent three days digging up the dam and searching for Virginia's remains.

The tip and the excavation both proved fruitless.

IN 1946
THIS MAN
KILLED
FIVE
PEOPLE!
...TODAY
HE STILL
LURKS THE
STREETS OF
TEXARKANA,
ARKANSAS!

Charles B. Pierce's

THE TOWN
THAT
DREADED
SUNDOWN

A TRUE STORY

An AMERICAN INTERNATIONAL Release

Starring

BEN JOHNSON
ANDREW PRINE · DAWN WELLS
as Helen Reed

Written by EARL E. SMITH
Produced and Directed by CHARLES B. PIERCE
Music by JAIME MENDOZA-NAVA
color by TECHNICOLOR®   **R** RESTRICTED

Released in 1976, *The Town That Dreaded Sundown* was based on the Texarkana Moonlight Murders thirty years earlier. Virginia Carpenter had known three of the victims. *Courtesy of Shreveport Journal.*

ZACHARY DIED IN 1980, and Hazel Carpenter passed away in 1985. As previously noted, in December 1948, Hazel bravely said, "I have accepted death in the past, and I can again, and would prefer that to some of the things that could have happened to her [Virginia]." The comment was perhaps too blunt for some folks' tastes, but it should be noted that Hazel was a longtime resident of Texarkana, a community that was still reeling from the Texarkana Moonlight Murders.

The Texarkana Moonlight Murders were a series of unsolved killings and violent assaults committed in the Texarkana area in the spring of 1946 by an unidentified suspect known as the Phantom Killer. The attacks occurred between February 22, 1946, and May 3, 1946, and then the perpetrator, like the culprit behind the Icebox Murders in 1965 (discussed later in the book), vanished.

The Phantom Killer's first two victims were twenty-five-year-old Jimmy Hollis and nineteen-year-old Mary Larey. The Phantom Killer wore a pillowcase over his head with holes cut out for the eyes. He fractured Hollis's skull with a pistol and struck and sexually assaulted Larey with the barrel of the pistol, but Larey escaped and they both survived. The first double-murder, which ended the young lives of twenty-seven-year-old Richard Griffin and seventeen-year-old Polly Ann Moore, happened four weeks later. The second double-murder, involving seventeen-year-old Paul Martin and fifteen-year-old Betty Jo Booker, occurred exactly three weeks after the first murders. In the last attack, which occurred almost three weeks after the second double-murder, a thirty-seven-year-old farmer named Virgil Starks was shot twice in the head while seated at his dining room table, and his thirty-six-year-old wife, Katie, was shot twice in the face but managed to flee the house and escape. Virgil died, and Katie survived. The Phantom killings stopped but were never solved. Virginia Carpenter had known three of the Phantom Killer's victims, and some investigators wondered if her disappearance was somehow linked to the gruesome murders in her hometown. The truth of the matter, however, is probably much simpler.

In 1948, amicable taxi driver Edgar Ray Zachary benefited from being the last person to see Virginia Carpenter alive and the only one to allegedly see her speaking with the two boys in the cream-colored convertible that the Denton Police Department never found. In 1957, Zachary benefited from the fact that a twenty-five-year-old mother of three couldn't risk rumors of being a sexual assault victim at a time when the stigma of being a rape (or attempted rape) victim could be detrimental to a woman's reputation and problematic in terms of her current and future employment prospects. Zachary's lawyer was making a show of dragging out the court proceedings, and the young woman simply wasn't interested in her name being made public.

This doesn't prove that Zachary was Virginia's abductor or murderer but lightning definitely struck twice for the amicable taxi driver, and though there was smoke on two separate occasions roughly nine years apart, investigators never proved fire.

8
WALLED KINGDOM

These days you can't throw a rock in Texas without hitting a truck with the Running W brand on it. The brand was originally registered by the one-million-acre King Ranch in South Texas on February 9, 1869, and used almost exclusively to mark livestock. But the new millennium saw the King Ranch join forces with the Ford Motor Company to create the King Ranch edition pickup truck, and the two iconic institutions have been *trucking* ever since.

Before the King Ranch was a Lone Star icon, however, many folks considered it a scourge.

The King Ranch's current webpage for Licensing/Partnerships states, "Running W stands for uncompromising quality, ruggedness, innovation, self-reliance, and authenticity." But in the 1930s, the Running W stood for something else. It symbolized what many South Texans called a "Walled Kingdom."

The Walled Kingdom was (and arguably still is) its own private empire. The King Ranch operated by its own set of rules, and the folks who lived outside it—including government officials—were basically treated like hirelings or peons. For decades, the citizens of the Lower Rio Grande Valley had requested that a hug-the-coast highway be run through King Ranch to spare people the extra fifty-mile trek it took to drive around it, but the "kingdom" had resisted. And over the years, a number of folks had gone missing there, but most of them were Mexican or Mexican American, so hardly anything was done about it.

The Blanton family after John and Luther vanished in the Walled Kingdom. *Courtesy of Valley Morning Star.*

In the late afternoon on Wednesday, November 18, 1936, fifty-three-year-old Myrtle Blanton waited on her husband, fifty-seven-year-old Luther, and son, twenty-four-year-old John, to return. Luther and Myrtle had a little plot of land in San Perlita, Texas, right next to the one-million-acre King Ranch, and their children lived nearby. John and his wife, Ruth, had a six-month-old son named Lawrence.

The Blantons were proud, hardworking farmers. They were respected by their neighbors, who, like most of the rest of the country, were still struggling though the Great Depression. Meat on the dinner table was a special occasion, and that's what Luther and John had set out to facilitate. Thanksgiving was still a week away, and thousands of ducks were passing through on their journey south for the winter, many stopping at a pond just a few hundred yards across the Walled Kingdom fence line. The Blantons were acquainted with some of the fence riders in that part of the gargantuan spread—what could it hurt? Luther and John crossed the three-strand barbed-wire fence with a double-barreled shotgun and three shotgun shells.

When it started to get dark and Myrtle still hadn't heard from her husband or son, she began to grow anxious. Had her husband and son gotten lost? Had they spotted a fence-rider and concealed themselves?

Though it was late, especially for duck hunting, Myrtle heard shots and thought her husband and son would be home soon. But then an hour went by and then another hour. Myrtle began to worry. She endured a virtually sleepless night.

When Luther and John didn't turn up the next morning, Myrtle assumed they had gotten arrested for trespassing. Myrtle had a neighbor drive her and her son Frank to the Willacy County Courthouse in Raymondville. It housed the county jail in its basement.

Myrtle soon discovered that her husband and son weren't there. When she contacted Willacy County sheriff H.T. Cragg, he was flippant about their whereabouts. Cragg performed a perfunctory search around that part of the King Ranch and said he didn't see anything. Later, a state patrolman named Jerry Modesette scoured the area around the pond and found duck feathers, cigarette butts and threads from torn overalls—threads that matched the denim overalls Luther and John had been wearing when they left.

Cragg searched again and found nothing else. Then, the Texas Rangers showed up and proceeded to spend more time looking like investigators than

Frustrated San Perlita citizens gather and threaten to invade the Walled Kingdom. *Courtesy of* Valley Morning Star.

really doing any investigating. The Blantons' neighbors grew frustrated. Longtime San Perlita resident J. Thomas Heath said it best: "When the Blantons had no troubles, we had no troubles. Now the Blantons are in deep trouble—and so are we." First, the Blantons' friends discussed "invading" the King Ranch near the fence line it shared with Luther and Myrtle. Then, over one hundred men gathered in San Perlita and challenged the Texas Rangers (who they believed were in the King Ranch's pockets), demanding that they be allowed to search the Walled Kingdom themselves. Myrtle defused the situation, asking the locals to give the Rangers a chance.

Luther and John Blanton were not the first folks to disappear inside the Walled Kingdom, just the first White ones. Reyes Ramirez and Jesus Rivera, a Mexican citizen, had vanished there less than a year before, and several more had reportedly been killed there over the years. In a December 14, 1936 *Life* magazine article titled "The Battle of the Fence," then owner and "boss" of the King Ranch Robert Justus Kleberg Jr. was asked to comment on the missing Blantons. His response was curt and dismissive. "It looks pretty hard to hold us responsible for people who crawl through our fence," he said. "We can't provide hunting for everybody."

Myrtle Blanton continued to press local authorities for answers, and the remaining Blantons started receiving death threats. In late January 1937, Frank received a letter informing him that "there is plenty of room for you where your dad and brother are." In March 1937, Frank's wife, Gladys, was attacked and beaten.

Myrtle later regretted any faith she had in local or state law enforcement officers. When the foreman of the King Ranch spread next to the Blanton's property passed away in mid-1937, Sheriff Cragg was one of his pallbearers. Of Captain William McMurray, the original Texas Ranger in charge of the investigation into the disappearance of Luther and John Blanton, Myrtle didn't mince words when Governor James V. Allred considered sending him back to the area. "Do not send McMurray," she communicated in a telegram. "I think he will cover up more than others can find." When Myrtle and the rest of the family hired private detectives, they were obstructed at every turn. When a private investigator named Louis LaMadrid seemed to be on the verge of solving the mystery, he was almost arrested three times in one day. Around 9:30 a.m. on Saturday, July 10, 1937, Texas Ranger Power Fenner took LaMadrid into custody in Willacy County for carrying "two, big six-shooters" in Cameron County. LaMadrid was transferred to Brownsville, and local attorneys secured him a $1,250 bond. LaMadrid was released at 5:10 p.m., and Ranger Fenner was waiting. At 5:11 p.m.,

Texas Ranger Power Fenner pulls a gun and raises it after local journalists take his picture. *Courtesy of* Valley Morning Star.

LaMadrid, who had previously been appointed deputy constable, was rearrested by Ranger Fenner for impersonating an officer. LaMadrid's attorneys immediately went back into action and secured him a second surety, this one for $60,000. It was posted by two prominent Valley men who were fed up with the Walled Kingdom's propensity to put its interests before the law. LaMadrid was rereleased that evening around 9:30 p.m. while another warrant was being prepared against him.

The message was clear: the private investigators the Blantons had hired to determine what became of Luther and John were to back off or else. LaMadrid confirmed this himself: "A trustee in the jail told me that I would be killed if I stayed in all night," he said.

When local journalists tried to get the details of LaMadrid's imprisonment, Ranger Fenner pulled a gun on them and attempted to disable their camera so photographs couldn't be taken. The attempt failed, and the photographer published the photograph in the *McAllen Monitor* newspaper. Fenner was subsequently dismissed from the Rangers, and LaMadrid was run out of the area and later reported to be out of the country.

Fence Riders are tough hombres on King Ranch. These are proud Mexicans, intensely loyal to their bosses and jealous guardians of ranch property.

THE BATTLE OF THE FENCE

THE King cattle ranch, in southern Texas, is the biggest in the country—about four-fifths the size of Delaware. Around it run 1,500 miles of wire fence to keep cattle in, trespassers out. On Nov. 18, Luther Blanton and his son Frank, truck farmers, crawled through the fence to shoot duck on the King Ranch. Shortly Mrs. Luther Blanton heard three shots and a neighbor's girl was so startled that she jumped off a fence post and tore her new dress. The Blanton men never came back from their hunt. In a day or two, the neighbors' concern became a furious conviction that hard-boiled King Ranch fence riders had murdered the Blantons for poaching. Plain Texans hate the King Ranch and its owners, the Klebergs. The Klebergs refuse to let hunters into their game-abounding land, refuse to let main highways go through their vast acres, and are politically a law unto themselves. Armed posses formed to invade the ranch and search for the Blantons or their killers. To the scene hurried Texas Rangers, more to keep the peace between citizenry and ranch than to find the Blantons in the dense scrubby woods. Requests for action went up to Governor Allred who kept clear of the affair. (Wise Texas governors usually leave the landed barons of South Texas to themselves.) The search went on in vain, the threat of war passed and the rangers kept one eye on the simmering citizenry, the other on the sky for buzzards who can find a dead body where men cannot.

Robert Justus Kleberg, Jr. is boss of King Ranch's 1,250,000 acres, its 125,000 head of cattle, its 500 employes. "It looks pretty hard to hold us responsible for people who crawl through our fence," he said of the Blanton case. "We can't provide hunting for everybody. The whole thing is a newspaper buildup."

The disappearance of Luther and John Blanton received coverage in the fourth issue of *Life* magazine on December 14, 1936.

A court of inquiry into the disappearance of Luther and John Blanton's disappearance was eventually granted and, later, a grand jury convened. But they were just for show. The district judge had already prohibited the local judge and grand jury from handing down murder indictments.

In late 1938, Myrtle sold her and Luther's place and moved to California. John's widow, Ruth, married a local named Orville May and remained in the area. May raised Lawrence as his own.

In 2001, Mona D. Sizer devoted the first chapter of her book, *Texas Justice: Bought and Paid For*, to a discussion of the Blanton disappearance. John Blanton's son, Lawrence, then sixty-five, wrote an epilogue to the account. In the epilogue, Lawrence discussed a deposition of a King Ranch employee that turned up years later in a deceased lawyer's office. The document directly addressed the deaths of Lawrence's father and grandfather. It stated that two King Ranch employees had discovered John and Luther at the pond on that November day in 1936 and attempted to take them into custody. It said that when Luther tried to resist, he was killed. And then John, no doubt upset, also struggled and was killed. According to Lawrence's mother, Ruth, the two men who dispatched the Blantons were subsequently transferred to work on a King Ranch property in South America.

If—as the November 23, 1936 edition of Harlingen's *Valley Morning Star* suggests—Luther and John Blanton were "swallowed" by the Walled Kingdom, some small satisfaction might lay in the knowledge that their unknown fates subjected the King Ranch to some level of bellyache. In 1940, the thoroughfare that the spread had always successfully resisted was cut through, severing but not spelling an end to the once unassailable domain. It's known as US-77, and every day, hundreds if not thousands of Ford King Ranch edition truck owners ply the route between Corpus Christi and Brownsville completely unaware.

9

TUGBOAT TERROR

After the M/V *Southern Cities'* next-to-last Gulf of Mexico crossing in 1966, its chief engineer, Frank McCarney, quit his post in Port Isabel, Texas. He vowed to never ship out with the *Southern Cities* again. He would later tell a Coast Guard fact-finding panel that even though the tugboat had been in "first class condition," he was "scared" of the vessel.

That fear probably saved McCarney's life.

On Saturday, October 29, 1966, the eighty-five-ton, 67-foot tugboat *Southern Cities* left Freeport, Texas, headed for Tuxpan, Mexico. The welded steel, diesel-propelled *Southern Cities* was towing a 210-foot-long, 40-foot-wide barge filled with thousands of fifty-five-gallon barrels of caustic soda and acid.

The *Southern Cities'* final radio communication was received early on Tuesday, November 1. The sender's last words were, "It looks like it will be the best trip yet."

But the port authority in Tuxpan—which is located on the Tuxpan River and is the closest port to Mexico City—never saw the *Southern Cities* arrive, and the barge was discovered adrift in the Gulf of Mexico, forty miles northeast of Tampico. The barge's cargo was still intact, but the tugboat was nowhere in sight. And the eight-inch-thick polypropylene towline that would have connected the *Southern Cities* and the barge was dangling from the barge undamaged.

Sometime after the *Southern Cities'* last optimistic radio message, a norther blew into the Gulf of Mexico, bringing winds of ninety to ninety-five miles per hour and raising the waves to sixteen to eighteen feet. A search for the missing tugboat began on Thursday, November 3 and lasted until Tuesday, November 8. Nine Coast Guard aircraft, including a specially equipped, four-engine Lockheed Hercules participated in the search, which covered eighty-four thousand square miles. A life preserver, a ring of life buoy and the tug's nameplate were eventually recovered at different spots in the vicinity of the *Southern Cities'* presumed route, but the vessel itself was never located. And the six-man crew, which included Captain Grady Reynolds of New Orleans; mate Victor L. Benton of Omega, Florida; deckhand George R. Johnson of Jacksonville, Florida; deckhand Buddy Lee of Perry, Florida; deckhand Tommy E. Roland of Perry, Florida; and engineer Clyde W. Sparkman of Houston, was lost at sea.

IN THE ENSUING INVESTIGATION, the details concerning some of the *Southern Cities'* Gulf of Mexico crossings explained McCarney's fear. Built in 1944, the tugboat was not used for anything other than inland service until July 1966, when the vessel's owner contracted to tow barges between Freeport and Tuxpan. On its first barge tow, the *Southern Cities'* automatic direction finder became disabled, and the crew lost its bearings. The captain contacted the Coast Guard, and the vessel was located well off course, approximately fifty-five miles north of Tampico. The Coast Guard helped guide the tugboat to Tuxpan, and the direction finder was replaced. On its second Gulf of Mexico crossing, the tugboat had problems with its generator, and the barge towline got caught in the tug's propeller. The *Southern Cities'* third trip to Tuxpan was uneventful, but its fourth (and McCarney's last), on October 8, 1966, was a nightmare.

The *Southern Cities* encountered bad weather including forty-five mile per hour winds and fifty-foot seas, resulting in "great quantities" of water leaking into the engine room. And neither the engine-driven bilge pump nor the electric bilge pump proved sufficient to mitigate engine room flooding. Then, the tug's electrical power failed, and Captain Reynolds was concerned about the main mast breaking and being carried away. He contacted the Coast Guard, and the USGC Cutter *Triton* escorted the *Southern Cities* toward its destination until the weather cleared.

When Coast Guard lieutenant commodore John D. Costello, the commanding officer of the *Triton*, later testified in an inquiry into the *Southern*

Cities' disappearance, he was blunt: "In my experience of going to sea I've never heard a master [captain] as frightened as Mr. Reynolds sounded," Costello said.

Coast Guard and National Transportation Board examinations both subsequently concluded that the M/V *Southern Cities* tugboat was vulnerable to the unpredictable conditions that vessels face on the open ocean and unsuited for service outside the harbors and ship channels of inland waters. The *Southern Cities'* final transport—like the SS *Marine Sulphur Queen*'s almost four years before it—was a voyage to oblivion.

10
BABY BRAY

In the late morning hours of Wednesday, June 29, 1955, twenty-year-old mother Verba Parrack let her boys go out to play in the family's modest South Oak Cliff backyard. Recently remarried, Verba kept a watchful eye on her twenty-two-month-old son, Gary DeWayne Bray; his five-year-old brother, Johnny Lee Bray; and their six-year-old stepbrother, Larry Keith Parrack. At one point, Gary DeWayne, a winsome, blond-haired, blue-eyed child who was about thirty inches tall and weighed twenty-nine pounds, stood at a fence in the Parrack yard and cried after his brothers when they went to play in a neighbor's yard. They returned and comforted him, and he went back to exploring his family's yard alone. At around noon, Verba stepped inside the house for a few minutes while Gary DeWayne was playing, and when she returned, he was gone. She reportedly called Johnny Lee and Larry Keith over, but they hadn't seen or heard anything.

Verba called the police, and authorities initiated an intensive search. The Parracks lived at 131 East Danieldale just off Highway 77, between Dallas and Lancaster. Almost 150 searchers combed over every inch of the Danieldale neighborhood and the surrounding fields for two days with no results. By the late afternoon of Friday, July 1, Verba had succumbed to nervous exhaustion and was admitted to Parkland Memorial Hospital. Dallas County sheriff Bill Decker said Verba had been hysterical all day as they worked on new leads for Gary Dewayne's disappearance. The toddler's father, Norman Lee Bray, a twenty-year-old cadet at Lackland Air Force Base in San Antonio, arrived that evening to speak with investigators and help with the ongoing search.

Sheriff Decker issued a missing persons bulletin, and by the weekend, local, state and national law enforcement agencies were searching for Gary DeWayne. Decker posted a horse-mounted deputy to patrol the area behind the houses on Danieldale.

Verba Parrack was released from Parkland over the weekend but collapsed on Monday, July 4, and was readmitted. Authorities pursued every clue, no matter how large or small, reexamining many locations, performing a house-to-house canvas, opening every icebox door, checking every ditch and storm drain, searching every pond and questioning the family's relatives in Oklahoma and elsewhere. Mrs. Parrack returned home on Thursday, July 7, to terrible news. There was no sign of her youngest son and no promising leads. Investigators suspected he was possibly snatched up by a sexual deviate or abducted by a love-starved, childless couple who decided to make Gary DeWayne their own.

On July 27, 1955, a boy matching Gary DeWayne Bray's description turned up in a church in Wilmington, Delaware, and Dallas County sheriff's deputy C.L. Lewis and Verba's husband, Travis A. Parrack, traveled there to see if he was Gary DeWayne. The toddler, who had been dubbed "Boy X," had blond hair and blue eyes and was the same height and weight as Gary DeWayne, but it wasn't him. Parrack was disappointed. "Now what do we do from here?" he asked of Deputy Lewis. "We're right back where we started."

On Monday, August 1, the local searches for Gary DeWayne resumed, and Sheriff Decker expressed frustration. "We're simply starting all over again," he said. A week later, on Gary DeWayne's second birthday, Verba baked a cake in hopes that her son would be there to eat it, but it went unserved. It was a grim setting.

"She wanted to bake the cake," Travis Parrack said, "but I told her it best that she didn't."

No one in the Parrack household ever baked another cake for Gary DeWayne Bray.

Weeks and months went by—and then years.

On February 24, 1956, an abandoned boy in Tucumcari, New Mexico, was mistakenly assumed to be Gary DeWayne. On February 26, 1957, a child was found murdered in a park in Philadelphia, Pennsylvania, and authorities there believed he might be Gary DeWayne. In mid-March, they acknowledged their error.

In May 2020, Gary DeWayne Bray's older stepbrother, Larry Keith Parrack, told me a lot of siblings and stepsiblings were shuffled in and out of their lives, and his dad had sent him to live with several different members of the family over the years. "It was an abusive environment," he said.

David remembered Gary DeWayne following him around a lot in his diapers, and he had fond memories of the deputy who patrolled the neighborhood on horseback. He was also able to add some details that the news reports missed. He said he remembered a car driving through an unpaved alley behind the houses on Danieldale the day Gary DeWayne disappeared. "I can remember it like it was yesterday," David recalled. "I saw it happen. It couldn't have been planned. They just stopped and grabbed him."

On the four-year anniversary of Gary DeWayne Bray's disappearance, a few local newspapers briefly discussed the toddler's fate, but a *Fort Worth Star-Telegram* headline put it best: "Child Toddled into Oblivion 4 Years Ago."

Gary DeWayne Bray has remained there ever since.

11

MISSING TRIO

On the mild winter midday of December 23, 1974, seventeen-year-old newlywed Mary Rachel Trlica, fourteen-year-old Leslie Renee Wilson and nine-year-old Julie Ann Moseley, all residents of Fort Worth, took Rachel's 1972 Oldsmobile to the Army-Navy Store at 601 West Berry to pick up two pairs of pants that Renee had on layaway. Renee changed into one of the new pairs of pants and placed her old pair in a bag with the other new pair. Then, they proceeded to the Seminary South Shopping Center (now La Gran Plaza) at 4200 South Freeway, parking near the Sears store's upper level on the east side of the mall.

Rachel and Renee's families had known each other for years, often going on family outings and camping trips together. Though married, Rachel was still a junior at Southwest High School. Her husband, Tommy, was a divorcee with a two-and-a-half-year-old son. Renee was a freshman at Southwest High School.

Described by her homeroom teacher as a conscientious student, Julie Ann was a fourth grader at B.H. Carrol Elementary School. She and her family lived at 3508 Gordon Street, just across from Renee's grandmother Mrs. J.E. Swinton. Renee spent a lot of time at her grandmother's, especially when her mother and father were at work. She knew the entire Moseley family, and some accounts indicate she had a crush on Julie Ann's fifteen-year-old brother, Terry. In fact, that morning Terry had reportedly given Renee a promise ring. The girls were expected at a birthday party at 6:00 p.m. that night, and Renee had told her parents she would be back at 4:00 p.m.

Though it was a Monday, school was out for Christmas break, and Rachel and Renee had some last-minute shopping to do. Julie Ann's mother, Rayanne, trusted Renee and let her daughter tag along because Julie Ann had complained about how boring it was to sit alone at their house. When the girls left to go shopping, Renee was wearing a yellow-green T-shirt with "Sweet Honesty" printed on the front.

Several witnesses remembered seeing Rachel, Renee and Julie Ann at Seminary South that day, but that was no surprise. The girls were young and vivacious and full of life. They would have grabbed attention in any setting, so it was strange when they spent an indeterminate period of time at the mall and then simply vanished.

When Renee didn't return at 4:00 p.m., her parents, Richard and Judy Wilson (of 5233 Frazier Avenue), grew concerned. At approximately 6:00 p.m., some of the girls' parents, including the Wilsons and Rachel's parents, Raymond "Cotton" and Fran Arnold (of 5748 Sixth Avenue), went to the mall and looked around. They found Rachel's car locked up tight with one gift inside.[38] The girls were nowhere to be found.

The girls' parents contacted the Fort Worth Police Department immediately, but officers didn't show up until 11:00 p.m.[39] And when they did arrive, they were surprisingly cavalier about Rachel, Renee and Julie Ann's absence. Despite vociferous protests to the contrary from the girls' parents—and some rather obvious non sequitur assumptions, like a nine-year-old would run away just before Christmas, a fourteen-year-old girl would split town after receiving a promise ring and a seventeen year-old would run away without her fairly new Oldsmobile with a nine-year-old girl in tow (and feel comfortable sneaking off right before Christmas)—investigators stated that they had no reason to suspect foul play and that they believed the girls were runaways. There was no immediate evidence of a struggle or witnesses to an abduction. And when Rachel's husband, Tommy Trlica, checked the car to see if anything was gone, he informed investigators that four items were missing from the glove compartment: three fifty-dollar bonds (purchased by him and his first wife) and a copy of his deceased parents' last will and testament. But Tommy wasn't sure when the items were taken and conceded that he might have misplaced them himself.

The Fort Worth Police were so certain that the girls might be with friends or that they had simply taken off that they neglected to dust Rachel's Oldsmobile for fingerprints.

The next day, Christmas Eve, a letter reportedly arrived at Rachel and Tommy's home at 3712 Minot Avenue in the Wedgewood East section of

Rachel Trlica   **Renee Wilson**   **Julie Ann Moseley**

Rachel Trlica, Renee Wilson and Julie Ann Moseley disappeared in Fort Worth, Texas, on December 23, 1974, and they haven't been seen since. *Wikipedia Commons*.

the city. It appeared to be from Rachel to Tommy, but the ballpoint-pen-performed handwriting looked to have been rendered hurriedly by someone who was right-handed—Rachel was left-handed—and Rachel's name was misspelled and corrected.

The envelope itself was also addressed to "Thomas A. Trlica" (in pencil), and Rachel always referred to her husband as "Tommy." Next to the ten-cent stamp in the right-hand top corner was a blurred U.S. Postal Service ZIP code number, 76083, which does not exist. And the number 3 in the nonexistent ZIP code appeared to be backward, indicating it might have been a faintly stamped 8 or the final two digits were transposed. (They were hand-loaded and stamped.) Also, a mailing label had apparently been removed from the exterior side of the back seal flap of the envelope—almost as if it had been mailed before.

The letter said, "I know I'm going to catch it, but we just had to get away. We're going to Houston. See you in about a week. The car is in the Sears upper lot. Love, Rachel."

Julie Ann's mother, Rayanne, said she "didn't put a lot of stock in the letter." Renee's mother, Judy Wilson, agreed: "It just doesn't make any sense." The message seemed to confirm the Fort Worth Police Department's initial assumption that the girls had run away, but investigators eventually questioned its authenticity. They also came to believe that if Rachel had been serious about leaving town, she wouldn't have taken either of the other two girls—especially nine-year-old Julie Ann—with her.

TOMMY TRLICA HAD BEEN engaged to Rachel's older sister, Debra, before he dated and married Rachel. At the time of Rachel's disappearance, Debra had reportedly been in a fight with her current boyfriend and was living with Rachel and Tommy. This arrangement made Tommy and Debra suspects. But Tommy had seemed legitimately bereft and immediately questioned the authenticity of the message from Rachel, specifically because of the author's spelling mistake. Rachel's name had been spelled "Rachee," and the author had gone back over the last cursive *e* with an *l*. It seemed unlikely that Rachel would misspell her own name, but detectives waved off this conclusion, suggesting Rachel might have made the mistake under duress.

If the U.S. Postal Service ZIP code was actually 76088, that meant it came from the Peaster, Garner or Brock areas. If the final two numbers were accidentally flipped and it was actually 76038, that meant it might have been stamped in Eliasville, north of Breckenridge and just southeast of Throckmorton, in West Texas—but that would have made it difficult, if not impossible, to arrive at the Trlicas' mailbox the day after the late afternoon or evening it must have been composed.

Several leads came in, but nothing useful materialized.

A night watchman at Alcon Laboratories Inc., at 6201 South Freeway, told detectives that the evening that Rachel, Renee and Julie Ann disappeared he saw two men and three girls in a car drive up to the entrance he was monitoring, but when he approached the automobile, it sped away. Authorities couldn't determine if it had anything to do with the disappearance.

A bus company employee said three girls fitting Rachel's, Renee's and Julie Ann's descriptions came in on Tuesday, December 24, between 8:00 a.m. and 11:00 a.m., inquiring about fares to Houston. But the three girls never purchased any tickets, and authorities had reservations about the reliability of the report.

At 1:00 a.m. on Thursday, December 26, a man called Rachel's father and said he had seen the girls and spoke with them at a record store at Seminary South on the day they disappeared. Another witness came forward and claimed he had seen the girls in a security patrol car that day. And later a truck driver called the Fort Worth Police and told them he'd seen the girls hitchhiking in Arkansas.

The missing girls' families began walking local creek beds and country roads, trying to help in any way they could.

On Saturday, December 28, Judy Wilson released a letter to the press. First, she addressed the girls themselves, stating that the families did not believe that the girls had "voluntarily run away, but if you have, we beg you to come home immediately or telephone so that someone can come after you. We are all behind you 100 percent and there is nothing that we will not do for you." Then, mindful of the possibility that the girls were abducted, Wilson also addressed their captors: "A special plea is made to any unknown person for these girls' release if they are being held against their will, so that they may be reunited with their loved ones."

On Tuesday, December 31, a hunter found women's undergarments in a field six miles west of Justin. When detectives arrived and investigated further, they found nothing linking the undergarments to the missing girls. Later in the day, a friend of Renee's father, Richard, informed the Wilsons that he had received a call at 6:00 p.m. from a girl identifying herself as Renee's friend, indicating that Renee, Rachel and Julie Ann would arrive on a Greyhound bus from Houston at 7:25 p.m. The Wilsons immediately contacted the other families, and they all made their way to the bus station and waited for the 7:25 p.m. bus. It arrived, but the girls didn't step off.

The families waited disappointedly at the bus station until 8:30 p.m. and then most headed home for what were no doubt low-key New Year's Eve observances. Richard Wilson and Tommy Trlica remained at the station for the next bus arrival from Houston at midnight. The girls weren't on that bus either.

The girl who had made the phone call to the friend of the Wilsons had identified herself as a friend of Renee's and shared her name, but when Judy Wilson asked friends of her daughter about the caller's name, they said they had never heard of her.

On Wednesday, January 1, 1975, Judy Wilson and other members of the missing girls' families spent part of New Year's Day meeting with J. Joseph, a Dallas psychic referred to the families by a local television personality. Joseph reportedly told the family members present that he sensed there was something wrong with the note that Tommy Trlica had received, that drugs were involved and that the girls were being held against their will.

By Tuesday, January 7, the ongoing story of the girls' disappearance—which had curiously never really been a big headline or front-page news in the *Fort Worth Star-Telegram*—had dropped to page eight of Section C. The headline read "Trio Missing for 2 Weeks," and the brief coverage below it noted that investigators were continuing to "follow up [on] what seemed to be a never-ending stream of dead-end leads."

In mid-January, a friend of the Wilsons started a reward fund at the Forest Hill State Bank to solicit information "leading to the recovery" of the missing girls. In late January, Paris, Texas residents Jesse and John McGee, both uncles of Renee Wilson, began distributing posters with details of the girls' disappearance in Paris and other major cities in Texas, Arkansas and Louisiana.

At 11:00 a.m. on Thursday, February 7, 1975, Rayanne Moseley received a call that she believed was from her daughter, Julie Ann. When she picked up the telephone and said hello, no one responded. She said hello repeatedly and decided to hang up, but then she heard a "low moan," and a voice said, "Mama."[40]

Rayanne asked the caller who she was, and the voice said "Mama" again.

Convinced she was speaking with her missing daughter but still wanting to be sure, Rayanne asked the caller if she was Julie Ann Moseley, and the voice at the other end said, "Yes."

"Listen," Rayanne continued. "If this is someone playing a joke, please stop. I can't take any more." Rayanne then asked the caller where she was, and she said she didn't know. The caller said "Mama" once more and then the call ended.

Rayanne screamed "Julie" into the phone repeatedly after the call was disconnected. She was badly shaken but later said the caller wasn't speaking "normally" and that she sounded like she was sick or drugged. But she was still willing to swear it was Julie Ann.

Soon after, all the missing girls' families were getting similar calls.

On Saturday, February 10, the Fort Worth Police conducted a trace of the phone at Renee's parents' home and pinpointed one of the calls to its place of origin.

The caller turned out to be a fourteen-year-old girl in North Richland Hills. She admitted to making three calls to the Wilson residence (but never spoke) and one call to the Moseley household, in which she told Julie Ann's older brother, Terry, that she was Renee Wilson. The prankster denied calling the Moseley residence at 11:00 a.m. on February 7.

At approximately 2:00 a.m. on Sunday, February 10, a gold sedan pulled up to a gas station at 3001 West Euless Boulevard. Three young White girls were in the back seat, and the driver was a Black man. The driver asked the gas station attendant if he could purchase beer, and the attendant told him it was after hours. As the driver pulled away, one of the girls in the back seat dropped a sheet of paper out of the car window. The attendant picked up the paper and called the police.

The sheet of paper was one of the "missing girls" flyers that Rachel, Renee and Julie Ann's families had been circulating. The address "1714 AP R.M. Blvd." was handwritten on it.[41]

Authorities researched the address and decided that it might refer to Randol Mill Road in Arlington. The Arlington Police assisted Fort Worth detectives in an examination of the general area and kept an eye out for a gold sedan at locations along the route. But there was no such address, much less apartments listed as AP or A9. They also never found the gold sedan.

In late February, police investigators received a tip that the bodies of the three missing girls were hidden beneath a bridge in the Port Lavaca area. The Port Lavaca Police checked the bridges and riverbanks and found nothing.

In mid-March, three clerks at a store inside the Seminary South Shopping Center told Rachael Trlica's mother, Fran, that an elderly woman had come by and claimed she had seen a man forcing a girl into the cab of a truck where there were already two other girls and a second man. Fran Arnold appealed to the clerks and the *Star-Telegram* to let the woman know to call and that "we would promise to keep her name a secret."

The source never came forward and identified herself.

When progress in the Fort Worth Police investigation grinded to a halt, some of the missing trio's family members hired Jon Swaim, a private investigator[42] who ran a local investigation firm called Special Services. Swaim created headlines and used the case's notoriety to force the Fort Worth Police Department into letting him examine the case files. By early April, Swaim reported that an unnamed source had informed him that the girls had been murdered and that their bodies were, as a previous tip had indicated, near Port Lavaca, lying under a bridge that spanned Hog Bayou along State Highway 35. The water under the area bridges was lower in April, and the resulting search party—which included the police, family members of the missing girls and one hundred volunteers—scoured the banks and waterways of the site a second time, but it was a difficult slog, and again, they found nothing. "You'd just have to see it to believe it," Swaim said. "You could dispose of hundreds of bodies in there and they would never come up."

In April 1975, the families' hopes of finding the girls alive "dimmed briefly" when a San Antonio fisherman found a human leg in a small local lake. Five bodies were recovered, but only two were female, and the girls were not among them.

Rachel's father, Raymond "Cotton" Arnold, succumbed to cancer on July 18, 1975, at the age of thirty-nine. By August, the families had been inundated with mail from seers, psychics and cranks from all over the world.

Judy Wilson said that she'd lost three of Renee's blouses, sending them off to mediums who requested a piece of her daughter's clothing to locate the girls' whereabouts. Approximately 60 percent of the psychics claimed that a "blue hippie van" was involved in the girls' abduction and that their captors had taken them north. One psychic sent Fran Arnold a map pinpointing the location of the girls in a shallow grave near a Mansfield Creek. Fran and Rachel's sister, Debra, walked several miles along the creekbank, and when they arrived at the spot where the bodies were supposed to be, they found the skull of a pig.

A short time afterward, a fifteen-year-old girl contacted Swaim with a tip about a man who had been making obscene phone calls to her and her older sister for over a year. When Swaim looked into the caller, he discovered that the man had worked at a store where Rachel Trlica had applied for a job shortly before her disappearance and that he had also lived in Rachel's parents' neighborhood at one time. Swaim coached the girl into meeting the caller on August 12 and then Swaim and some of his employees detained the suspect until the Fort Worth Police arrived to arrest him.

While in police custody, the suspect admitted to making numerous obscene phone calls to several of the women who had applied to the store (he got their phone numbers from their job applications), but he denied having anything to do with Rachel, Renee and Julie Ann's disappearance and agreed to take a polygraph test.

In March 1976, a Honolulu psychic contacted the Fort Worth Police and told them that the girls were deceased and that their bodies had been dumped near an oil well. The prediction led authorities to an oil field in the Amity community near Rising Star, but all the investigators found was another dead end. Later that year, Swaim received an anonymous phone call from a man insisting he could lead him to the girls but refusing to discuss whether they were dead or alive. "He told us it is a friend of his who can tell us where the girls are," Swaim said, "if, number one, the reward money will be paid and, number two, if he can get full immunity from any prosecution of any criminal act that he may have been involved in with the girls."

Swaim said the unidentified party also insisted that he be able to surrender directly to the district attorney's office with no law enforcement personnel involved.

When the unidentified informant phoned a second time, he reportedly sent Swaim to seventeen different payphones in Fort Worth before he would discuss a deal. Swaim attempted to arrange a meeting with the caller, but the man refused.

If Swaim's anonymous tipster ever contacted him again, it never made the newspaper. The purported seventeen-payphone straggle he described was also conspicuously reminiscent of a *Dirty Harry* (1971) plotline, and the girls' families eventually began to question Swaim's credibility.

In September 1978, Schepps Dairy in Dallas announced a reward program for information in resolving major unsolved crimes in Fort Worth. Years earlier, after a Schepps Dairy convenience store clerk was murdered during a robbery, the dairy posted a reward for information, and the reward led to the arrest and prosecution of the parties involved. Fort Worth police captain Roy Tate announced that the program would focus on one case at a time but listed several high priority cases that would be forwarded to the administrators of the Schepps program. The

Private investigator Jon Swaim was hired to find the missing trio and later died under suspicious circumstances. *Courtesy of* Fort Worth Star-Telegram.

list of victims included twenty-one-year-old Becky Martin, whose body was found on March 27, 1973, in a culvert just west of Fort Worth; seventeen-year-old Carla Walker, whose body was found in a culvert near Lake Benbrook three days after she was abducted from a local bowling alley on February 27, 1974; Rachel Trlica, Renee Wilson and Julie Ann Moseley; twenty-five-year-old June Ward, whose nude body was discovered a day after she disappeared on February 18, 1977; seventeen-year-old Lecia McGee, whose body was discovered in the trunk of her car on January 23, 1978; and twenty-four-year-old Paula Jean Davenport, whose decomposed body was discovered in a wooded area on the east side of Fort Worth on April 28, 1978. It was later determined that Davenport had been shot in the parking lot of a bowling alley, also located on the east side of town.

For a brief period, Lecia McGee's murder was investigated in connection with Rachel, Renee and Julie Ann's disappearance, because, like Rachel, Lecia also attended Southwest High School, and Lecia had her hair done at the same beauty parlor where Rachel, Renee and Julie Ann had theirs done years earlier. McGee's murder was later investigated in connection with the murder of Davenport because their cases had similar details and both had been murdered at different locations from where their bodies were discovered.

On October 19, 1979, police were called to Jon Swaim's apartment on the east side of Fort Worth around 2:30 p.m., after Swaim's landlord found him semiconscious. According to police officials, when officers arrived,

Swaim refused to be taken to a hospital, so they were forced to leave. At approximately 11:45 p.m., Swaim's sister and brother-in-law went to check on him after failing to reach him by phone. They discovered Swaim's dead body on his living room floor. Medical investigator R.O. Medford determined that Swaim had been dead for several hours.

Swaim's death was deemed the result of a drug overdose and was later ruled a suicide. But not everyone agreed with the final determination. Swaim's ex-wife had remarried the day before he died, and his detective agency was struggling financially, but one local attorney said that even though Swaim had telephoned him intoxicated several times in the weeks leading up to his death, he didn't sound suicidal. "Swaim was the sort of man you would think would like to have taken ten people with him when he went," the local attorney said.

Gary Davis, a bail bondsman and former eight-year employee of Special Services, suggested that it was no surprise that Swaim's private investigation firm was struggling. He claimed that Swaim had actually spent $20,000[43] of his own money working on the disappearance of Rachel, Renee and Julie Ann because he believed the girls were still alive.

Interestingly, the "voluminous" files Swaim was said to have kept—including those regarding the girls' disappearance and several files pertaining to members of law enforcement in Fort Worth—were reportedly burned by his ex-wife, as per his funerary instructions. So, his demise created suspicions, and some parties wondered if his death was the result of suicide or something more sinister.

ON NOVEMBER 1, 1980, the body of a young woman, aged fourteen to twenty, was discovered face-down in a patch of grass off the shoulder of Interstate Highway 45, just north of Huntsville, Texas. She had been sexually assaulted vaginally and anally with a large blunt instrument and then strangled to death. Her remains were compared with physical descriptions of Rachel Trlica but were not considered a match.[44]

In early March 1981, Brazoria County authorities discovered three human teeth in clumps of dirt near Alvin. They got in touch with the Fort Worth Police Department, and within days, Fort Worth detectives were at the site assisting in the excavations. For one month, the Fort Worth Police, Brazoria County deputies and a number of Brazoria County jail trustees conducted an intense search of an overgrown swamp area four miles south of Alvin. They uncovered nineteen human teeth, the right side of a jawbone, four spinal bones, two tattered pairs of girls' pants and a high school drama book.

In the end, the investigators were able to solve the mystery of two missing girls, but neither were Rachel, Renee or Julie Ann. The remains were those of two girls from Dickinson, Texas: fourteen-year-old Georgia Geer and twelve-year-old Brooks Bracewell. Geer and Bracewell had disappeared just a few months before Rachel, Renee and Julie Ann, on September 9, 1974.

ONE OF THE BIGGEST stories in the country in 1974 involved a missing young woman, but it was not Rachel, Renee or Julie Ann. It was Patty Hearst, granddaughter of American publishing magnate William Randolph Hearst.

Abducted on February 4 by a left-wing group known as the Symbionese Liberation Army, nineteen-year-old Hearst was reportedly brainwashed and tortured. A little over two months later, she was making propaganda statements for her captors and had been photographed with an M1 Carbine gun during a robbery in San Francisco. The biggest story of the year, however, was Richard Nixon's resignation on August 7. It disgraced the American presidency and the Republican Party, which had carried 70 percent of the votes in Tarrant County in the most recent election.

Carla Walker disappeared in Fort Worth on February 17, 1974, and her body was found in Benbrook three days later. *Courtesy of* Fort Worth Star-Telegram.

By the time Rachel, Renee and Julie Ann disappeared, the public was in no mood to fret over teenagers who the Fort Worth Police Department characterized as runaways. The day-to-day atmosphere was one of gloom, and the Watergate trial, which was one of the most publicized legal proceedings in American history, was playing out just when the girls disappeared. In addition to this, the city of Fort Worth was dealing with a damaging scandal of its own.

In September 1974, civil service officials had voided the results of the police department's sergeant's exam after it was discovered that several officers had been given the results of the test beforehand. By that December, civil service commissioners and city council members were tossing the incident around like a hot potato, because, politically speaking, no one wanted to run afoul of their own police force. So, when Rachel, Renee and Julie Ann vanished, the Fort Worth Police Department was dealing with serious morale problems, and the community was frustrated and sullen and possibly singularly disinclined to be interested in the disappearance of three "runaways." This might also explain the *Fort Worth Star-Telegram*'s marginal coverage of Rachel, Renee and Julie Ann's disappearance. People were no doubt disturbed by the incident, but it appears that very little or not enough was done about it. And this is disturbing, because it came only seven months after the abduction and murder of Carla Walker.

On February 17, 1974, seventeen-year-old cheerleader Carla Walker and her boyfriend, quarterback Rodney McCoy—both Western Hills High School students—attended a Valentine's dance. They partied with friends afterward and then stopped by a popular bowling alley so that Walker could use the restroom. When the two returned to their vehicle, an unidentified party attacked them as they got inside, grabbing Walker and striking McCoy over the head with a gun. When McCoy regained consciousness, he was covered in blood from his head wound, but he proceeded straight to the Walker residence to let her family know what had happened. Carla's parents called the police, but they were unable to find her.

Carla's body was discovered in a muddy culvert near Benbrook Lake three days later. She had been injected with morphine and kept sedated for two days while her captor (or captors) repeatedly beat and raped her and then strangled her.

In February 1989, Fort Worth detective George Hudson contacted NBC's *Unsolved Mysteries*, hoping the show could help with the long-running investigation and shine light on the missing trio's disappearance. If the program examined the incident, its producers must not have been comfortable with the case's ratings potential. It was never explored in one of the program's broadcasts.

For decades, the Fort Worth Police Department continually reached out to medical examiners in a five-state area, inquiring about unidentified Jane Does but never found matches for Rachel, Renee or Julie Ann. And every couple of years a local newspaper or news station revisited their story, soliciting tips or witnesses, to no avail.

In recent years, investigators reportedly pulled DNA from the letter Tommy Trlica received on the morning of that fateful Christmas Eve, but they never found a match.

In March 2016, James "Ice" McAlpin, a former pimp and convicted murderer doing time in a correctional center in Marianna, Arkansas, for killing his prostitute girlfriend, inserted himself into the narrative. McAlpin murdered the prostitute girlfriend, known by her street name, Mercedes, in 1992, but Arkansas investigators still hadn't determined her real identity. After twenty-four years, she was still referred to as a Jane Doe.

When investigators approached McAlpin about Mercedes's real identity, he said he would provide her name if they paid him. To date, McAlpin hasn't been remunerated for the information Arkansas investigators requested, but he did discuss Mercedes's past. McAlpin said Mercedes had been on the street since she was sixteen and was pimped out in Fort Worth and Dallas. He also said Mercedes "grew up friends" with three girls who were kidnapped from a mall in Fort Worth in the 1970s: "These girls were like sisters to Mercedes. We used to visit them. They grew up in captivity in the Dallas/Fort Worth area, sometimes in the same town where their parents were. By the time they were adults, they were willing members of the stable. The younger girl died giving birth to a child."

Arkansas authorities familiar with McAlpin claim he's a compulsive liar and say they're not even sure he knows Mercedes's real identity. But his reference to three girls whose circumstances possibly resembled those of Rachel, Renee and Julie Ann is worth noting, even in terms of the horrific implications the suggestion portends.

One special investigator (who requested that his name be withheld) submitted a completely different narrative. After investigating the case off and on for forty-five years, he argued that the most important question isn't who took the girls but why the girls might have wanted to leave. According to him, at least two of the girls' family lives were largely dressed up in newspaper accounts to suggest they were members of normal, happy families, when, in fact, nothing could have been farther from the truth.

Cotton Arnold was reportedly "abusive" to Debra and Rachel. Julie Ann Moseley's mother, Rayanne, allegedly had substance abuse issues. Tommy Trlica was a recently divorced father of one and a trust fund wastrel when he courted and became engaged to Rachel's sister, Debra, who was working as an exotic dancer. Then, by the time Tommy met, dated and became engaged to Rachel, Cotton Arnold was dying with cancer, and Tommy bought Mr. Arnold's failing business—thereby procuring Cotton and Fran Arnold's blessing to marry seventeen-year-old Rachel. Furthermore, Rachel's medical records reportedly suggest that Rachel was pregnant when she disappeared, and it was common knowledge that Tommy didn't want any more children. And multiple sources hinted that Rachel and Tommy weren't getting along.

This investigator also said that although the media coverage then and ever since usually made a special point to mention that Julie Ann's older brother, Terry, had given Renee Wilson a promise ring, she had actually fallen for Terry's friend Vernon Beaty and that the Fort Worth Police interviewed Beaty because the girls had actually met him at the Seminary South Shopping Center the day they vanished. Beaty denied involvement in the trio's disappearance, and virtually every party still invested in Rachel, Renee and Julie Ann's disappearance—including major media outlets—prefers the "normal, happy" homelife backdrop behind discussions of the mystery.

On September 21, 2020, Glen McCurley, a seventy-seven-year-old Fort Worth resident, was arrested for the rape and murder of Carla Walker. New DNA procedures linked McCurley to Walker's bra, and Fort Worth detectives said he confessed during questioning.

RACHEL TRLICA'S YOUNGER BROTHER, Rusty Arnold, was eleven when his sister disappeared. "Not a day goes by that I don't think about her," he says. "And her two friends."

Now fifty-seven, Rusty administers Missing Fort Worth Trio, a Facebook page devoted to discussion of their fate. He's been investigating the case for decades and has no plans to quit. Sometimes, he admits, it's too much:

> When we were kids, we used to go camping at Benbrook Lake a lot, me, Rachel, Debra and my mom and dad. And sometimes the Wilsons would come as well. For the last couple of years, I'd been trying to find the creek we camped on. It was called Rocky Creek and I just couldn't find it. I had looked for it several times in my boat. So, the last time I went camping with my family, I finally found Rocky Creek. I drove up to the exact spot we had camped at…and I just lost it. I had finally found it. I started crying. I hadn't been there in years, but it brought it all back.

Rusty stays in touch with members of the other families and acknowledges that it's highly unlikely that his sister Rachel or the other girls are still alive. "I'm at least ninety-nine percent sure," he said. "But there's that one little part of me, that one percent, that still holds out."

IN THE MONTHS AFTER Rachel, Renee and Julie Ann disappeared, Tommy Trlica left Fort Worth and moved to the Throckmorton area, where he had some family. The ZIP code in this area matched that of the transposed code on the letter Tommy received on Christmas Eve. Was Tommy Trlica involved in the disappearance of Rachel, Renee and Julie Ann? Or did the girls actually run away, as the cops originally suspected?

Was 1974 an off year for the Fort Worth Police Department?[45] Did the investigation into the girls' disappearance suffer due to a local testing scandal or general resentment toward free-spirited young people in an era of Nixonian gloom?

Why was the Fort Worth Police Department so quick to dismiss Rachel, Renee and Julie Ann as runaways? And how could they forgo taking fingerprints from Rachel's Oldsmobile, the best opportunity for physical evidence in the crime?

Why did the missing trio's disappearance remain a missing persons case for eight months? And why did the anonymous caller who contacted Swaim say he would surrender to the Tarrant County district attorney but not the Fort Worth Police?

The disappearance of Rachel Trlica, Renee Wilson and Julie Ann Moseley on December 23, 1974, is the oldest missing persons case in Tarrant County. And time has hardly diminished the pain and anguish their families have been forced to endure.

Will the mystery of the missing trio ever be solved?

12
HOOD'S HUBRIS

Born in Kentucky, John Bell Hood graduated from West Point at the age of twenty-two. After soldiering in California and Texas for the United States, he joined the Confederacy as a cavalry captain and became one of the most rapidly promoted leaders in the Confederate military. As colonel of the Texas Fourth Infantry, he garnered distinction on a dozen different battlefields, and in the Seven Days Battles—near Richmond, Virginia, from June 25 to July 1, 1862—he acquitted himself legendarily in the eyes of his comrades by leading his brigade in an astonishing charge that broke the Union line. But while Hood emerged from the carnage without a scratch, every other officer in the brigade was killed or wounded. Hubris was one of Hood's calling cards, and it was first displayed in Texas.

In the summer of 1857, Hood was an enthusiastic young brevet second lieutenant of the Fourth Infantry stationed at Fort Mason in Central Texas. Tall, blonde-haired and blue-eyed, Hood cut a fine figure, and his enthusiasm for military service—and military distinction—was singular.

In early July, he was sent out by the post commander, Major George H. Thomas, to investigate "Indian" activity reported by a scouting party led by brevet second lieutenant John T. Shaaf. On the morning of July 5, Lieutenant Hood and renowned Delaware tracker John McLoughlin set out with twenty-five Second U.S. Cavalry troopers. They traveled south until they reached the Llano River and then headed due west. Three days in, they camped at the ruins of Fort Terrett,[46] which had been abandoned three years earlier due to the installation of outposts farther west.

A cavalry hunting party, dispatched to supplement the patrol's store of hard tack and bacon, cornered a bear in a local cave and slew it, but not without incident. The leader of the hunting party, a Sergeant Deacon, had fired on the bear in its subterranean den, but his shot only wounded it. Forced to flee, Sergeant Deacon led the pursuing bear out of the cave, where it was slain by Deacon's cohorts. In his flight, however, Deacon turned a knee. Lieutenant Hood's detachment enjoyed bear for dinner and the next morning's breakfast but lost two of its number to early attrition. The wounded Sergeant Deacon was forced to return to Fort Mason, and Corporal Henry Jones was sent to accompany him.

Proceeding from the former Fort Terrett, Hood's patrol was unable to locate any traces of recent indigenous tribal activity or traffic, but the young lieutenant was "bent on action"[47] and veered northwesterly. The detachment encountered several old trails and eventually turned west. After a number of long, punishing days navigating a bleak desert wasteland, Lieutenant Hood's patrol discovered evidence of a recent Comanche campsite at the mouth of Kiowa Creek.

The Comanche contingent, which included fifteen to twenty horses (and at least the same number of men), was reckoned to be three days ahead. And though his men and horses were already struggling with the summer heat, Lieutenant Hood decided to give accelerated pursuit.

The Comanche party turned south and then back east, and G Company discovered further evidence of its trail a couple of miles south of Lipan Creek:

> *Hood continued the chase, following a line of water holes that were from 35 to 50 miles apart, a course that marked some of the main Comanche trails into Mexico. The dogged cavalrymen rode rapidly south under a brutal July sun. Unfortunately, few of the water holes yielded palatable water. The smell was so bad at several of the watering places that the men had to hold their breath as they drank from the stagnant pools. At the scum-covered, brackish ponds the soldiers filled their canteens and the sleeves of all waterproof coats; they could take no chances: even if the water was bad, each water hole might be the last.*[48]

The young lieutenant forced his troopers forward, the patrol's blue uniforms gray from caked dust, and yet each soldier was hesitant to allow complaints air from his parched throat. When voices were finally heard, they came in the form of cries—for water. According to trooper H.G. Rust, who was interviewed by *Hunter's Magazine* in 1911, the going became increasingly grim. "It was the hottest weather I ever experienced, and our horses suffered beyond measure. We struck a fresh Indian trail which, after following it all day, seemed to lead everywhere and nowhere in particular. Later developments led some of us to believe that the Indians had discovered us and were leading us around over a most desolate region, where there was no water, in order to reduce us to a famished condition so that we might become an easy prey."[49]

BY COMANCHE DESIGN OR not, seven of Lieutenant Hood's cavalrymen were rendered ineffective due to their own exhaustion or fatigue or that of their horses and were left behind.

On the morning of July 20, G Company of the Second Cavalry discovered a recently abandoned campsite at a watering hole a few miles north of the Devil's River. Smoke still rose from the remains of the fire, and it was clear that a second indigenous contingent (including some Lipan Apache) had joined the initial Comanche party, putting the overall number of combatants at well over fifty. At this point, Lieutenant Hood was given an obvious opportunity to reexamine the situation his detachment found itself in. His men were exhausted and suffering from extreme thirst. The Comanche had meandered into the setting almost leisurely; the Second Cavalry had dashed headlong in a grueling chase to catch up, physically debilitating the troops and drastically overworking the horses. Though most of the accounts of the engagement then and now suggest Hood and his men were outnumbered two to one, they politely ignore the fact the young lieutenant had run his troops ragged and incapacitated at least seven—so they were actually outnumbered three to one.

Hood assessed the increasingly perilous situation and chose to proceed.

After what was left of the detachment finally partook of a decent water source near the head of the Devil's River, the Comanche were spotted on a high ridge. Lieutenant Hood initially assumed they were Tonkawa because they had raised a white flag. A group of Tonkawa was expected at a reservation near Camp Cooper (to the west) soon, and they had been instructed to display a white flag to request peaceful passage.

Forming a line and leading sixteen men forward with guns at the ready (McLoughlin remained behind with the pack mules), Hood proceeded cautiously in case the white flag was a ruse. When the dwindled remainder of Company G moved within thirty yards of the Comanche, five warriors advanced toward the cavalrymen and tossed the white flag (a bedsheet) aside. Squaws traveling with the Comanche braves simultaneously set brush fires on the perimeter. It was a trap, and (as Hood would later detail in his memoirs)[50] the Comanche rose up from all sides: "Thus began a most

Before John Bell Hood was a legendary Civil War general, he was an overly ambitious, reckless brevet second lieutenant in the U.S. Cavalry. *Wikipedia Commons*.

desperate struggle. The warriors were all painted, stripped to the waist, with either horns or wreaths of feathers upon their heads; they bore shields for defence [*sic*], and were armed with rifles, bows and arrows. The quick and sharp retort of our rifles, the smoke and cracking noise of the fire, together with the great odds against us, the shouts of the soldiers and the yells of the Indians, betokened the deadly peril from which seemingly naught but a miracle could affect our deliverance."

ARMED WITH RIFLES, PISTOLS, shotguns and bayonets, Hood's command arguably benefitted more from superior firepower—and luck—than divine intervention. Company G withstood the initial ambush and then fell back to a better defensive position. An arrow pinned Hood's left hand to his bridle, but he removed the arrow himself and kept fighting. The brush fires made it difficult for the cavalrymen to train their gunsights on combatants at a distance, but this cut both ways, forcing the Comanche to engage Hood and his men at close quarters, where the latter's revolvers wrought bloody havoc.

Sustaining several casualties and numerous injuries, the Comanche force subsequently ended the onslaught and began gathering their dead and wounded. Hood's company was in horrible shape and vulnerable to a second attack, but the Comanche departed the field and headed toward the Rio Grande. Weary of another ambush, Hood and his men held their positions until 10:00 p.m. Physically spent and extremely dehydrated, they camped on a bank near the Devil's River. Hood dispatched a messenger to Camp Hudson to secure medical aid and supplies.

Privates William Barry and Thomas Ryan were killed during the melee, but the former's body was never recovered. Four members of Company G (including Hood) were also wounded. The Comanche force suffered nineteen casualties, and twice that number were wounded. The Battle of Devil's River would afford Hood his first bit of notoriety and lead to his promotion to first lieutenant in 1858.

Brevet Major General David E. Twiggs, known for his own brand of recklessness in the Mexican-American War, praised Hood's engagement with the Comanche as a "gallant" affair, lauding the young lieutenant and his men. Others, however, wondered if his impulsiveness hadn't earned him censure:

> *It is beyond doubt that Hood displayed exceptional bravery and leadership skills that made him legendary among the rank and file during the American Civil War. He had a knack for inspiring men to phenomenal feats. However,*

Hood's poor judgement in pursuing the numerically superior Indian party over the desolate landscape impractically jeopardized the lives of his men. The ambush at Devil's River was an indicator of his recklessness that became notorious during the later part of the American Civil War. Unfortunately, he was not commanding company-size formations and suffering the loss of a few men—over 6,000 would fall at Franklin owing to his rash orders— but instead ordered thousands of ill-fated Confederate soldiers to their deaths owing to his characteristic impulsiveness and lack of better judgment.[51]

The standard reports were filed, battle renown was achieved and Hood's military career was on its way, but the accounts were clearly kind to the victors—or survivors—depending on how you look at it.

In the final days of Hood's pursuit of the Comanche party, he was driving his men an average of fifty miles a day in suffocating desert heat without fresh water, or even potable water. Almost every report of the engagement glosses over or ignores the fact that Hood abandoned the troops who fell out along the way—and no account mentions what happened to them. There is no indication that they were searched for, much less reclaimed. In his memoirs, Hood notes that he continued the pursuit of the Comanche "in the conviction that we could live for a short time wherever Indians could subsist," suggesting that it was a matter of principle and that he believed that White men could do anything the indigenous peoples in the area could do. But this observation ignored the plain reality that, especially at the accelerated pace G Company maintained to catch the Comanche party, Hood was asking the soldiers under his command to do more than their foe—and with no water. His ambition and the shared glory his exploits showered on his fellow officers and immediate superiors blinded them all. Company G didn't just lose two men in the Battle of Devil's River—they lost nine. The seven troops Hood abandoned likely succumbed to dehydration, malnutrition or hostile encounter. Historian Gregory Michno's *Encyclopedia of Indian Wars: Western Battles and Skirmishes, 1850–1890*, states that the seven cavalrymen "began to drop from exhaustion and were left behind," never to be seen or heard from again. They were committed to oblivion by their own commander, who seemed to be more interested in glory than the welfare of his troops.

In 1987, the Val Verde Historical Commission placed a historical marker commemorating the Battle of the Devil's River near the ghost town of Juno (two miles north of the intersection of SH162 and RR189). The marker doesn't mention the men consigned to oblivion, but it's hard to not think of them when you stare out from that spot at the desolate, unforgiving landscape.

13

CAT GOT THEIR TONGUES

On the evening of Tuesday, March 5, 1957, William and Margaret Patterson apparently abandoned their home at 3000 Piedmont Drive in El Paso and vanished, leaving behind almost all of their possessions. The next day, Cecil Ward, Mr. Patterson's best friend, discovered Patterson's Cadillac in the driveway of his auto repair shop, the Ward Motor Clinic.

Ward was confused. He had been at the Patterson place with his wife on Monday and spoke with William—also known as Pat—on the phone the night they disappeared. Pat hadn't said anything about his car needing work. When Pat's friend Doyle Kirkland showed up at Ward's shop that morning around 8:00 a.m., he informed Ward that the Pattersons had decided to take a vacation and enlisted him to drop off the Cadillac to have a few things fixed. Kirkland, who ran Duffy's Photo Service—a direct competitor of Pat and Margaret's Patterson's Photo Supplies—told Ward he'd been at the Patterson's home the previous night helping William work on his boat. Ward grew suspicious and called the police.

When El Paso police officers arrived at the Patterson residence, the couple was gone, there were dirty dishes stacked up in the kitchen sink and clothes were laid out in their bedroom. The only outfits or clothing missing, however, were dozens of the couples' expensive suits and dresses that had been left at the cleaners with no instructions for them to be stored or picked up. And all of the Pattersons' luggage was still at the house. Pat's business associates, including Kirkland and Pat's accountant, Herbert Roth, insisted Pat and Margaret's vacation had been a spur-of-the-moment decision.

Days and weeks passed, and there was still no sign of the Pattersons. When a satisfactory explanation wasn't proffered after six months, people started asking questions. On Thursday, August 15, 1957, El Paso County sheriff Jimmy Hicks issued a national all-points bulletin. At that point, the Pattersons' personal histories were examined.

Pat had grown up in one of the rougher parts of Chicago and learned that a clever tongue was as handy as quick fists. He left home in what his father later called a "teenage pique" and kicked around the country. He worked several odd jobs and then became a carnival barker, "'conning' the country boys to whistle at the hootchie-kootchie girls and watch the 'geeks' eat raw chickens."[52] Later, Pat worked as a salesman for the Nedell Manufacturing Company of Chicago, but he had bigger plans. Deprived of the finer things in life as a child, he was obsessed with having them as an adult. It was during these early days that he met and married a beautiful slender redhead named Margaret. She worked at the Hotel Vendome in Evansville, Indiana.

Pat was a good talker and a great salesman. He was peddling aging reflex-type cameras when he discovered photography, and it would be a part of his life from that point forward. He became a good photographer and subsequently made street photography his side hustle.

In 1940, Pat and Margaret moved to El Paso and got stuck there during World War II. They lived in a dilapidated trailer house, and Pat worked as a street photographer and a security officer for a local nightclub. Soon, Pat had two shutterbugs performing the street photography work for him, and he approached a local moneyman about a loan. He had no security to put up for the loan, but the "burly, nimble-tongued ex-carnie"[53] reportedly inspired confidence. Pat received funding, and things really started to take off.

In a few years, Pat had Herbert Roth (originally from New Jersey), a successful, connected local accountant, handling his books and Dave J. Smith working as his attorney. And Kirkland had become acquainted with Pat through a dynamic of friendly competition. Pat and Margaret were soon the owners of Patterson's Photo Supply Co. at 133 North Main Street.

By 1956, Patterson's Photo Supply was doing $350,000 worth of photography business,[54] and Pat and Margaret were living large. They had a posh house in the Kern Place section of El Paso and owned a 1956 Cadillac, a fancy (now iconic) Volkswagen Karmann Ghia sports car, an RV and a top-of-the-line motorboat that Pat took on fishing trips to Florida, Mexico and the West Coast. They traveled and wore flashy clothes (Margaret had two mink coats) and expensive jewelry. They had achieved the American dream, but as was (and still is) so often the case, there were nightmarish downsides.

William and Margaret Patterson vanished in El Paso on March 5, 1957, and their disappearance wasn't reported for six months. *Courtesy of the Daily News.*

Pat was having affairs, and Margaret, who reportedly enjoyed more than the occasional drink, was drinking heavily to deal with her husband's philandering. The Pattersons had never had children, so Margaret doted on her yellow-and-white-striped cat, Tommy—so much so that his victuals sometimes included caviar.

Like many examples of the nouveau riche, however, Pat was also incredibly and annoyingly cocky. "Sure," Cecil Ward said six months after the Pattersons' disappearance, "he was loud-mouthed and a braggart, but also a pretty good guy. He lived it up, but I guess he was making up for all those years when he didn't have anything."

In February, the month before the Pattersons disappeared, Pat's arrogance got him into some trouble just across the Rio Grande. He was in a swanky Ciudad Juarez nightclub having a drink with a beautiful twenty-year-old bar girl named Estefana Morfin. When Pat's waiter refused to serve Estefana because the business owners didn't like the "help" getting inebriated on the clock, Pat got angry and loudly expressed his displeasure. Two bouncers promptly advised him to pipe down, and Pat refused. A small brawl ensued, and Pat was "banged up," but it supposedly didn't go any further.

ON MARCH 15, 1957—AFTER Cecil Ward continued to raise questions about the Pattersons' whereabouts and the couple's abandoned residence had been searched and deemed suspicious—accountant Herbert Roth received a mysterious telegram from Dallas. It was apparently a message from Pat, instructing Roth to lease the Patterson residence, sell the RV, make Kirkland the manager of Patterson's Photo Supply and serve himself as the chief executive of the booming business. The telegram's origin was traced to a pay station near Dallas Love Field Airport, but the sender could not be identified. And the telegram, it's timing and the message itself were very suspicious. Pat never sent telegrams. He preferred to handle business over the phone. And the person on the sending end of the telegram got Pat's middle initial wrong.

Meanwhile, Roth began driving the Pattersons' Cadillac, and the fancy Karmann Ghia sports car was used by Patterson's Photo Supply personnel.

When El Paso County sheriff Jimmy Hicks began investigating the Patterson disappearance in the summer of 1957, Roth, Kirkland and the Pattersons' lawyer, David J. Smith, all clammed up. And Pat's father and sisters—who curiously accepted Roth and Kirkland's explanation that the Pattersons had abruptly decided to take a long trip without any of their luggage or their wardrobe (which was still at the dry cleaners)—requested that the search be called off.

The only concerned parties besides the sheriff's department were Cecil Ward; Pat's mistress, Estefana Morfin; and the El Paso National Bank. Ward believed the Pattersons were dead because they wouldn't have left without telling him or his wife, especially since they had visited with them twice in the days before they disappeared. Morfin offered to put up her Jurarez home and her $1,600[55] American bank account to help fund the search. And in light of the ongoing questions regarding the Pattersons' absence, the El Paso National Bank grew increasingly uncomfortable with processing Patterson's Photo Supply checks with Roth's signature on them.

Then, there was a break in the case.

The November 1, 1957 edition of the *El Paso Herald-Post* summed it up best: "Tommy the Cat was brought back today into the mysterious disappearance of Mr. and Mrs. W.D. Patterson as the silent but most substantial evidence that the Pattersons faded out unaware they were not soon to return—if ever."

TOMMY THE CAT THREW a serious monkey wrench into the works of the Pattersons' business associates and family members who were claiming that Pat and Margaret were on an "extended vacation." Pat's sister, Mildred Boris (of Chicago), had actually inquired into the welfare of Margaret's beloved feline in conversations with employees at Patterson's Photo Supply. She was informed that Margaret had made arrangements for Tommy to stay at the next-door neighbor's while she and Pat were away—but this turned out to be a flagrant prevarication.

The Pattersons' only next-door neighbors were Nathan and Natalie Sherwin of 2940 Piedmont Drive, and no one had contacted them about the unexpected Patterson vacation or caring for Tommy. "When we learned that Mr. and Mrs. Patterson were away," Mrs. Sherwin said, "we still did not know Tommy had been left behind. The first time we knew Tommy was there was when my small son saw Tommy and came and told me, 'Tommy is home!' I went to see, and there was Tommy. We know Tommy well." The notion that Margaret would have left Tommy behind or left Tommy alone with no provisions for his well-being was absurd to Sherwin. "Margaret never would have done that intentionally," Sherwin continued. "Margaret and Pat loved animals like parents love a child—and gave the cat the same care you would expect parents to give a child."

Tommy apparently survived on his own until Herbert Roth rented the Patterson residence to a lieutenant colonel named Philp Belson (stationed at Fort Bliss) in July 1957. The Belsons took Tommy in and took care of him until he bit one of the Belson children. When the Belsons took Tommy to the Cady Animal Hospital at 2101 Texas Street, the veterinary staff recognized the feline. Tommy had been there dozens of times, and when he arrived with the Belsons, "he purred his delight" at being back among friends. Tommy was often boarded at the Cady Animal Hospital when Pat and Margaret were on vacation.

Tommy the cat was problematic in the cover-up that sprang up regarding William and Margaret Patterson's deaths. *Courtesy of* El Paso Herald Post.

Pat's sister, Mildred Boris, and his father, seventy-five-year-old Luther Patterson, initially indicated they would request an investigation, but the new year saw them change their minds. Mrs. Boris was bothered by the shenanigans regarding Tommy but not enough to request an inquiry into her brother's disappearance. And when the Cady Animal Hospital contacted Patterson's Photo Supply about the boarding fees, an employee gruffly denied that Tommy was the Pattersons' cat. Luther and Mrs. Boris gave no reason for changing their minds and curtailing efforts to resolve the Pattersons' undetermined fate. In fact, when Boris was telephoned for comment, she seemed eager to end the conversation but made a couple of brief comments. "We have no intention of doing anything at all about it," she said. "We'll just wait and let them come back when they want to."

Tommy the cat's abandonment was the only evidence of foul play, but even though one of Margaret's closest friends said that "Margaret would no more have left Tommy uncared for than a mother would have abandoned an adored baby," it wasn't enough.

On January 1, 1958, the El Paso National Bank began refusing to honor checks drawn on Patterson's Photo Supply's $30,000 business account. On January 10, the Photo Supply company was placed in receivership at the request of Eastman Kodak, Hornstein Photo Sales (of Chicago) and Pat's father, Luther. Herbert Roth was named the receiver.

When the one-year anniversary of the Pattersons' disappearance came around, the *El Paso Times* published "The Case of the Vanishing Pattersons," summing up the status of the informal investigation. Tommy the cat was "involved in a legal battle between the veterinarian taking care of it and Herbert Roth." Pat's boat was rotting in the yard of a former employee. The local judiciary was saying it had no plans for a court of inquiry unless the sheriff's department requested one, and the sheriff's department was claiming it couldn't request one unless a member of Pat or Margaret's family requested it—and Tommy didn't count.

Within a week, a letter Pat had supposedly sent to Estefana Morfin entered the conversation. The April 1957 correspondence purportedly indicated that Pat would be back before Morfin's birthday (April 29), but Pat never showed. A week after the letter was mentioned, a preliminary hearing on the missing Pattersons commenced in the thirty-fourth district court in El Paso. Several tidbits of new information came to light. Among them, (1) Pat's Cadillac had been thoroughly cleaned before it was dropped off at Ward Motor Clinic; (2) no one—including Doyle Kirkland, who claimed Mr. Patterson had called at 3:00 a.m. and instructed him to drop it off before he left—could identify who actually dropped it off; (3) the letter Morfin allegedly received was not in her possession (and later she denied ever receiving a letter from Pat); and (4) Art Moreno, Pat's right-hand man at Patterson's Photo Supply, said that Pat and Margaret had argued frequently before they vanished. "Their life was not pleasant," Moreno said. And he believed Pat wanted to get away "because of the unpleasantness with his wife."

The preliminary hearing was an interesting step, but investigators still couldn't demonstrate evidence of foul play, key witnesses refused to testify and the Pattersons' former business associates were still assuring anyone who would listen that nothing was amiss. District attorney William F. Clayton agreed to seek a court of inquiry—but only if one member from each side of the Pattersons' families requested it.

ON WEDNESDAY, APRIL 9, 1958, three boys who were hunting frogs found the body of a slender partially nude redheaded woman under some brush in a eucalyptus grove near Burlingame, California. The woman was found lying on her side with a black and white tweed coat draped over her shoulders. The Burlingame Police said her hands had been bound by a sash cord, her panties stuffed down her throat and her decomposed body looked like it had been placed there about a year ago. They considered the possibility that the redheaded Jane Doe might be Margaret Patterson

Some El Paso residents believed that the Pattersons were abducted by a UFO (*Mysterians* movie poster circa 1959). *Portal to Texas History*.

and contacted the El Paso Police Department. When newspapers around the country began publishing pictures of Margaret alongside stories about the body found in Burlingame, Margaret's former landlord and landlady in Evansville recognized her. The body in Burlingame later turned out to be somebody else, but the landlady had already contacted Margaret's relatives. Margaret had four sisters and two brothers residing in Illinois, Indiana, Kentucky and Missouri. They had not heard from her in over twenty years.[56]

"We thought she was dead," said Katie Wahl, Margaret's sister in Illinois. But now that Wahl and Margaret's other siblings realized that their sister hadn't been dead before but might now be dead—and then found out the corpse in Burlingame wasn't her, and she was still missing—they took an active interest in helping find her. Katie Wahl soon made the trip to El Paso to see what was what.

On Friday, April 18, Wahl met with Sheriff Jimmy Hicks and then Harold Long, the court-appointed attorney engaged in receivership action against Herbert Roth's incarnation of Patterson's Photo Supply, which was turning handsome profits. On the evening of Saturday, April 19, Pat's relatives were suddenly on board with a court of inquiry as well. "It's time something was done," Luther Patterson conceded over the telephone from Illinois.

On Sunday, April 20, however, Sheriff Hicks killed himself in front of another officer in a local hotel room.

By THE TIME LUTHER Patterson arrived in El Paso on May 28, 1958, to testify before an official board of inquiry proceeding devoted to the disappearance of his son William and his daughter-in-law Margaret the following week, the El Paso County Sheriff's Department had already concluded that Sheriff Hicks's demise was in no way connected to the Patterson disappearance. And, though in mid-April Luther had indicated that it was "time something was done," he had changed his mind and again felt nothing should be done. He cheerfully told newspaper reporters that his son was alive. "Pat was tired and wanted to rest," Luther said. "There has been no foul play. Pat will be back when he is ready."

On June 2, 1958, the board of inquiry into the Patterson disappearance commenced, and eighteen witnesses testified. Then, another dubious letter, reportedly received by Pat's lawyer, David J. Young, the week before, was introduced for consideration:

Dear Dave,

I want [sic] *you to handle this matter for us. We will not be back to El Paso and by the time you get this we will be out of the country and no body* [sic] *can find us. We want Art, Doyle and Herb to each have a fourth of the business, the fourth must be divided equal among the other employees at the store. See that Art gets the house and furniture. Doyle is to get the cabin, tools, boats, and the Cadillac. Keep the Vw* [Volkswagen] *for the business, as well as the lots. I expect you to be fairly paid for all the trouble. Margaret wants her account to go to CYO. Art Moreno, Doyle Riley and Herb Roth should make a good trio to run the store from now on.*

Yours truly,
W.D. Patterson

The letter upended the entire board of inquiry. Why were the popular Pattersons never returning to El Paso? Why hadn't any correspondence been received from Margaret? Why hadn't Margaret cosigned the letter, which read like a last will and testament? Had Margaret Patterson been murdered?

After the missive was conveyed, Luther Patterson held forth again. "Pat will never be back," he said. "My son has his reasons. I believe Margaret may be ill; but you can rest assured Pat is taking good care of her."

Wahl and Ruby Kiefer, another of Margaret's sisters, who had chosen to attend the inquiry, were not so sure. "The letter makes me believe more than ever that our sister is dead," Wahl said. "I fear she has been killed."

The board of inquiry was suspended indefinitely on June 5, 1958. Luther Patterson visited the Cady Animal Hospital on June 12 and verified that the cat reported to be Tommy was actually him. "That's Tommy," Luther confirmed. "No question about it."

Luther decided to remain in El Paso, but he didn't take Tommy with him.

The dubious letter that sabotaged the 1958 board of inquiry was later determined to be a hoax.

In August 1962, Patterson's Photo Supply was sold.

IT REQUIRES THE PASSAGE of seven years for an absent party (or, in this case, parties) to be declared legally dead. So, on the seventh anniversary of the Pattersons' disappearance, their former business associates and some family members (notably, Luther Patterson[57])—who had all along claimed Pat and

Margaret were living it up somewhere outside the country—became keen on having them declared dead.

A new court-appointed attorney for Pat and Margaret requested a delay to examine the four-hundred-page court of inquiry from 1958, but the declaration of death was eventually approved. In late 1964, William and Margaret Patterson were pronounced legally dead, and Roth was named the administrator of the estate. His testimony in the declaration hearings was almost comical. He insisted that all leads in the Patterson disappearance had been investigated "diligently" over the past seven years and that he now believed the Pattersons were deceased.

Twenty years later, a man who had presumably been involved in a cleanup of the Patterson residence after Pat and Margaret's disappearance spoke with the El Paso County Sheriff's Department. His name was Reynaldo Nangaray, and he said he hadn't come forward sooner because he had been an undocumented immigrant at the time. Now a U.S. citizen, Nangaray told investigators that he had found blood on the concrete of the Patterson's garage and a piece of human scalp attached to the propeller of Pat's boat. Nangaray also said he witnessed one of Pat's associates removing a bundle of bloody sheets and stowing them in the trunk of a car. An indictment was prepared, but it never went anywhere

Nangaray died in a car accident two years later.

The Patterson investigation was officially reopened in 1984, 2005 and 2011. Outside of Nangaray's testimony in 1984, no new useful leads appear to have been acted on. It brought *El Paso Herald-Post* writer Marshall Hail's March 3, 1964 comments to mind:

> *According to Hercule Poirot, the private eye in Agatha Christie's mystery yarns, there are three kinds of disappearances: amnesia or loss of memory (rare), voluntary disappearance, and murder with successful disposal of the body.*
>
> *Amnesia can be ruled out, since the chance of two persons being stricken at the same time is doubly remote.*
>
> *Voluntary? Why would the Pattersons give up their friends, home, the prosperity that had eluded them so long? Why would they remain completely silent for seven years, without a word to their kin?*
>
> *Murder?*

If murder, the Patterson's killer(s) definitely got the "with successful disposal" of the bodies requirement right. And Nangaray might have witnessed that part. But the question becomes why?

Some theories suggest that the Pattersons were Cold War spies and that Pat or Margaret (or both) might have drawn the wrong kind of attention to themselves. The Photo Supply would have been the perfect front, and all kinds of interesting things were going on at Fort Bliss.

Some people believe Pat was killed for his missteps in the Juarez nightclub in February 1957 and that Margaret was a collateral victim. Some folks believe Pat might have killed Margaret after an argument over Estefana Morfin and left the country to evade prosecution and imprisonment. Some people wonder if Margaret didn't kill Pat for his indiscretions and go on the lam herself.

And still others maintain that the Pattersons were abducted by a UFO.

Active engagement of any angle of the investigation in the Pattersons' disappearance seems to lead to more questions than answers. And almost everyone who could answer those questions is now long gone, including Tommy the cat.

They say he eventually died of heartache at the Cady Animal Hospital.

FORGOTTEN MASSACRE VICTIMS

On Thursday, November 21, 1946, the Woman's Foundation of New York announced that it was awarding the Hogg Foundation for Mental Hygiene[58] at the University of Texas a one-year grant totaling more than $10,000[59] to establish community development projects in several small cities and towns around the state. The first communities chosen were Waco, Beaumont, Corpus Christi and a little town called Slocum in East Texas.

Since the Slocum program was aimed at helping a six-community region, with Slocum at its center, it was called the Slocum Rural Family Life Project, and it commenced in early December 1946 under the direct supervision of the Hogg Foundation. The area was strictly segregated, and the members of the Black population who participated did so at the Union Hope Baptist Church, just east of Slocum. The oversight of the program fell to Joseph William "Joe" Hassell, the White superintendent of the Slocum schools, and his wife, Dora, a White home economics instructor.[60] A steering committee for the White participants was established fairly quickly and uneventfully, but a committee for the Black citizens was an entirely different matter. When Joe and Dora Hassell addressed interested parties in the Black community, they did not receive the response they anticipated. According to Mr. Hassell, "They were met with a sea of cold indifference and almost stony silence."

A superficial examination of Mr. Hassell's remarks might lead one to believe that this instance of chilliness sprang up spontaneously and from nothing in particular—or that the reception that the Hassells faced evidenced a serious lack of appreciation from the primary beneficiaries of the program. There were no doubt people in the Slocum community who might have agreed with that assessment.

But there was much, much more to the story.

THE DAWN OF THE twentieth century in Slocum, Texas, saw some Black citizens considerably propertied and a few owning stores and businesses. The Reconstruction period after the Civil War (which mightily frustrated many of the White citizens of Anderson County) was over, and some Black people who had been born into slavery had established footholds in the local economy. The Holley family, for example, apparently owned the community's only general store and hundreds of acres of rich farmland.

This alone, in parts of the South, would have set the stage for White violence. But in the Slocum area, which included the small communities of Ioni Creek, Percilla, Aldenbranch and Denson Springs, there were other issues. When a White man named Reddin Alford quarreled with Marsh Holley over a disputed debt, there were hard feelings and frustration lingered. When Black Galveston native Jack Johnson[61] pummeled the Great White Hope, Jim Jeffries, to become the world heavyweight boxing champion in early July 1910, many White people construed the pride that Johnson's victory inspired in Black people as "uppity" behavior. And when a regional road construction foreman put Abe Wilson (a Black man related to the Holleys by marriage) in charge of rounding up help for local road improvements, a White half-renter[62] named Jim Spurger was infuriated and started causing trouble.

Wild rumors began to circulate, suggesting that local Black citizens were planning an uprising. Racist malcontents manipulated the local White population, and, on July 29, White hysteria transmogrified into bloodshed.

Goaded by Spurger and others, hundreds of White citizens from Anderson County and the surrounding counties converged on the Slocum area armed with pistols, shotguns and rifles. That morning, near Sadlers Creek, they fired on three young Black men headed to feed cattle, killing eighteen-year-old Cleveland Larkin and wounding fifteen-year-old Charlie Wilson. The third, eighteen-year-old Lusk Holley, escaped, only to be shot at again later in the day while he; his twenty-year-old brother, Alex; and their friend William Foreman were fleeing to Palestine. Alex was killed, and Lusk was wounded. Foreman ran for his life. Lusk pretended to be dead so that a group of twenty White men wouldn't finish him off.

White mobs marched through the area gunning down unarmed Black folks at will. A thirty-year-old Black man named John Hays was found dead in a roadway, and twenty-year-old Sam Baker was shot to death in front of his house. When three of the Bakers' relatives (Dick Wilson, his son Jeff and seventy-year-old Ben Dancer) attempted to sit up with his body the following night, they, too, were murdered in cold blood. According to a report in the *Galveston Daily News*, bloodstains at the residence indicated that they were shot on the front porch and then dragged inside.

In addition to the Anderson County murders, which occurred near the county line, Will Burley was killed just south of Slocum in Houston County. One later report of the massacre indicated that every Black person "caught" between Slocum to the north and Houston County Farm Road 227 (from Grapeland to Augusta) to the south was slaughtered.[63]

According to the August 1 edition of the *Newark Daily Advocate*, the mobs traveled from house to house, shooting Black people who answered their hails and slaughtering more while they tended their fields.

Almost every early newspaper report on the transpiring bloodshed in and around Slocum portrayed the Black citizenry as the instigators, implying that the local White community was simply defending itself. But these accounts were gross mischaracterizations. When District Judge Benjamin H. Gardner closed saloons in Palestine and ordered local gun and ammunition stores to stop selling their wares on July 30, it was not to stop a Black uprising but to defuse what the *Galveston Daily News* called an indescribable, one-sided "reign of terror" characterized by "a fierce manhunt in the woods" and resulting in bullet-riddled Black bodies everywhere.

When reporters gathered on July 31, up to two dozen murders had been reported and dozens more were suspected, but local authorities had only collected eight bodies. Once the carnage had begun, hundreds of Black people had fled to the surrounding piney woods and local marshes. And by the time the Texas Rangers and state militia arrived, there was no way to estimate the number of Black people who had died.

On August 1, a few Texas Rangers and other White men gathered up several Black bodies and buried them (wrapped in blankets and placed in a single large box) in a large pit four miles south of Slocum. Some reports suggest that the unmarked mass grave was full of dozens of corpses because law enforcement personnel kept coming out of the woods with more bodies. Farther north, Marsh Holley was found on a road just south of Palestine. He was terrified and begged the authorities for help, requesting that he be taken to the county jail for his own protection.

AFTER THE FIRST SEVERAL murders, the Black community began fleeing en masse, but this didn't stop the White mobs. Most of the victims were shot in the back. Two bodies found near the town of Percilla (in Houston County) still had travel bundles of food and clothing at their sides.

Anderson County sheriff William H. Black said it would be "difficult to find out just how many [Black people] were killed" because they were "scattered all over the woods." He also admitted that buzzards would find many of the victims first, if at all. Certainly, with the arrival of the press—and after early attempts at spinning the news reports to portray the Black victims as armed insurrectionists had failed—the guilty parties engaged in damage control efforts. After the initial bloodlust subsided, some of the transgressors returned to the murder scenes to remove the evidence of their crimes. But in terms of the official narrative, Sheriff Black was unequivocal. "Men were going about killing Negroes as fast as they could find them," he told the *New York Times*, "and, so far as I was able to ascertain, without any real cause."

"These Negroes have done no wrong that I can discover," Black continued. "I don't know how many [White people] were in the mob, but there may

The Slocum area of Anderson County harbors at least two mass graves, if not more, and when they are uncovered, they will yield images like this one from the Spanish Civil War. *Courtesy of Mario Modesto Marta.*

have been 200 or 300. Some of them cut telephone wires. They hunted the Negroes down like sheep."

According to the local law enforcement leaders on hand at the time, eight casualties was a conservative number. Sheriff Black and others insisted there were at least a dozen more and some reports suggest there might have been hundreds more. Some witnesses counted twenty-two casualties. Elkhart native F.M. Power said there were thirty "missing negroes." Slocum-area resident Luther Hardeman claimed to have knowledge of eighteen casualties, and that's the original number reported by the *Galveston Daily News* and the *New York Times* (on July 31)—but the body count seemed to shrink as the massacre's publicity grew. A reliable fatality count was soon impossible, especially with the perpetrators covering their tracks. And dead people weren't the only folks becoming scarce; the surviving Black community members began to disappear as well. It was one thing for them to return to their homes or their daily routines after the odd murder or infrequent lynching of a friend or loved one—Black folks in the South were not unused to that. But a localized campaign of genocide in which executioners surrounded them and cut phone lines to prevent them from getting help? That was not something Slocum-area Black people could easily relegate to a list of bygones.

If the proverbial water under the bridge was red with blood, home was no longer a place to return. And with a large contingent of the Black community running for their lives, many uncounted victims went unidentified and unreported. The arrival of the Texas Rangers and the state militia stabilized the situation—or at least made it safe enough for the remaining Black people to pack their belongings and leave without being fired on.

When a *Galveston Daily News* correspondent visited Lusk Holley and Charlie Wilson on July 31, they were both suffering from incredible levels of pain due to the gunshot wounds they had received. The writer reported that their injuries would be "relieved only by death unless medical attention is speedily afforded." Wilson had a fractured thigh, damage to one ankle and serious chest wounds. Holley had eight to ten pieces of buckshot in his lower left abdominal area and damage to one arm. Physicians had perfunctorily treated their wounds when they were first discovered two days prior, but not since.

Wilson told the *Galveston Daily News* correspondent that he had recognized two of the assailants during the first shooting on July 29. Holley said that after he had been wounded in the second shooting later in the day, a different group of White men had come upon him while he pretended to be dead. He said he recognized the voice of a prominent local farmer named Jeff Wise, who deemed his and his brother's apparent deaths "a shame" as he passed by.

In the weeks and months following what came to be known as the Slocum Massacre, the Black population made a mass exodus, leaving homes, properties and businesses behind. And that was fine with their White neighbors, whether they were participants in the bloodshed or passive bystanders.

The Black corpses scattered all over the Slocum area of southeastern Anderson County were being disposed of, and the perpetrators of the carnage were making themselves scarce or were too many in number and too diffused in terms of geography to round up, so Judge Gardner made a tough decision. Instead of waiting for the proverbial dust to settle, he decided to arrest the suspects he could and charge them with the murders they could immediately prosecute before all of the evidence and any more of the suspects disappeared. At the initial grand jury hearing, nearly every remaining Slocum resident was subpoenaed. Some residents refused to testify and were arrested. Judge Gardner told the all-male, all-White jury that the massacre was "a disgrace, not only to the county, but to the state" and it was up to them to do their "full duty."

According to the August 2 edition of the *Palestine Daily Herald*, Judge Gardner attempted to clarify the charges and the issues at hand, explaining various statutes to the jury. He said that even if there had been threats or conspiracies "on the part of any number of Negroes to do violence to white persons, it would not justify" vigilantism. "The law furnishes ample remedy," Gardner continued. "There is no justification for shooting men in the back" or "killing them in their houses."

When the grand jury findings were reported on August 17, several hundred witnesses had been examined. Though eleven men were initially arrested, seven were finally indicted, including Isom Garner, B.J. Jenkins, Steve Jenkins, Andrew Kirkwood, Henry Shipper, Curtis Spurger and Jim Spurger; only Kirkwood was immediately granted bail. No one was ever indicted for the deaths of John Hays or Alex Holley.

In the end, two cases involving the Slocum Massacre moved forward, one based on killings in Anderson County and one involving the murder of Will Burley in Houston County.

On November 14, 1910, the defendants in the Houston County case (Jim Spurger, Isom Garner, Andrew Kirkwood, William Henry, B.J. Jenkins and Henry Shipper) were arraigned, and each pleaded not guilty to the charge of first-degree murder. The presiding judge denied every defendant except Shipper bail. Shipper's bail was set at $5,000,[64] and his family and friends—O.M. Betsill, J.T. Gilmore, Thomas F.L. Hassell, O.A. McDaniel, J.D. McKeen, Mac Reed, J.J. Shipper and E.M. Shipper—put up their lands and properties as his surety.

On Wednesday, December 12, the defendants in the Anderson County case were arraigned, and Judge Gardner, on his own motion, announced the trial venue would be changed to Limestone County unless the attorneys for both the state and the defendants agreed to a different location in the counties of Navarro, McLennan, Williamson, Travis or Harris.

Judge Gardner preferred Navarro County, but he also liked Freestone County because the court met there the first Monday in January. The attorneys for the state and the defendants got together and decided on a venue in Harris County. The indictments languished in Harris County, and the cases were never prosecuted.

In the meantime, the personal holdings of many Slocum area White citizens fortuitously increased.

The abandoned properties of the Black citizens were absorbed or repurposed as the remaining White population saw fit. Many Black landowners were either dead or missing, and their land titles were vacated or revised. And then a 1913 fire at the Anderson County Courthouse conveniently destroyed many of the original titles, so the revisions couldn't be examined or questioned. The standard southern Anglo-centric order in Slocum was restored.

On April 24, 1929, a tornado rolled through Slocum, leveling the town, killing seven and injuring twenty. Organizations from all over East Texas went to great lengths to raise money for the victims and help the town get back on its feet. Though the Slocum Massacre's casualties were far greater and its Black community's forced migration was arguably just as landscape-altering, the twister overshadowed the localized genocide of 1910, and the atrocity remained largely ignored for over a century.

A Black Huston-Tillotson College professor named Ernest E. Neal eventually joined the Slocum Rural Family Life Project as an intermediary, and the Black participants, who had initially been "quiet and withdrawn in interactions," began to open up. In May 1947, the second year of the program, Neal noted talk of a "racial conflict" that had occurred in Slocum that the White citizenry "would like to erase from history": "No one seems to remember exactly when it occurred or what it occurred about. But it did

On January 16, 2016, the Slocum Massacre historical marker became the first state marker to specifically acknowledge racial violence against Blacks in Texas. Pictured in the foreground from left to right are Daisy Joe (with cane), author E.R. Bills, Constance Hollie-Jawaid and Carolyn Phillips. Joe, Hollie-Jawaid and Phillips are all descended from victims of the massacre. *Photo courtesy of Andrew Brosig.*

happen, and several Negroes were lynched. The people don't like to talk about it. But a few Negroes and Whites still remember the incident and the bitter feelings that lingered long after the incident passed."

So effective was the selective memory or collective amnesia in Anderson County and Texas in general that Neal's notation of this incident—the Slocum Massacre—was the first official mention of the atrocity in the three decades since it transpired.

Neal's predecessor, Joe Hassell, was born in Palestine, Texas, on February 21, 1891. His wife, Dora, was born in Norman, Oklahoma. Joe Hassell would have been nineteen when the Slocum Massacre occurred, but there is no evidence to suggest that he took part in the bloodshed. But Thomas F.L. Hassell—one of the guarantors of indicted suspect Henry Shipper's bail—was Joe's uncle. So, even if Joe Hassell didn't take part in the Slocum Massacre and perhaps wasn't even in the area when it occurred, it strains credulity to suggest that he wouldn't have heard of the bloodshed later or been aware of it at the time.

Thirty-six years had passed since the massacre, and it is doubtful that any Black participants in the initial Slocum Rural Family Life Project meeting would have recognized Joe Hassell, but they might have recognized his name. Or they might have been seized by the incredible irony of a White man in the Slocum community actually standing in front of them and professing an interest in their well-being after the White men who had eradicated whatever level of progress and prosperity Black people had achieved by late July 1910 suffered no consequences.

ON MARCH 30, 2011—AFTER a two-part exposé by Tim Madigan[65] appeared in the *Fort Worth Star-Telegram*—the Eighty-Second Texas Legislature adopted House of Representatives Resolution 865 (HR 865, filed by Representatives Marc Veasey[66] and Lon Burnam on March 11), acknowledging the Slocum Massacre.

After a long, hard-fought battle with the Anderson County Historical Commission, a state historical marker commemorating the 1910 Slocum Massacre was dedicated a half mile south of Slocum on FM 2022 on January 16, 2016. It lists the names of the original, officially acknowledged victims of the atrocity—which is good, because their bodies have never been recovered—but it doesn't acknowledge the other victims of the bloodshed. Apart from the unmarked pit containing the remains of at least six victims who the Texas Rangers supervised the burial of on August 1, 1910, three other unmarked mass graves have been mentioned, but only one has been located. It sits on private property off Anderson County Road 1208 and is said to contain sixteen to fifty-five bodies.[67] Another unmarked resting place in a forgotten cemetery on high ground just off Anderson County Road 1206, is believed to contain more bodies. The oral tradition passed down among members of the Black community has always suggested the actual number of men, women and children who perished in the Slocum Massacre was over two hundred.

Unlike the State of Florida, however, which has conducted an official investigation of the Rosewood Massacre,[68] and the State of Oklahoma, which has conducted an official investigation of the Tulsa Race Massacre,[69] the Lone Star State, to date, has not mustered the sense of justice, moral courage or political will to officially investigate the Slocum Massacre, much less to locate or acknowledge the actual number of its victims. So, most of them remain nameless, faceless and consigned to oblivion.

"It's a travesty," says Constance Hollie-Jawaid, a descendant of victims of the Slocum Massacre and the primary force behind the Slocum Massacre historical marker. "Some of my ancestors are piled up like animals in unmarked mass graves, but no one seems to care. Some people in this area even seem proud of it."

15

PORT LAVACA PUZZLE

WANDA LEE ANN PRIDDY

On Tuesday, August 29, 1978, Fred Priddy reportedly returned to the residence he shared with his twenty-year-old wife, Wanda Lee Ann Priddy, at 220 South Nueces in Port Lavaca, at 6:30 in the morning. He worked the graveyard shift at a chemical company in Palacios. He was tired but not so sleepy that he didn't notice that something was wrong.

Wanda's car was out front, but their front door was unlocked. Priddy checked every room in the residence, but Wanda was nowhere to be found. Yet her purse and car keys were still on the kitchen table. It didn't make any sense.

Priddy called the police, but the investigation led nowhere. There were no signs of a struggle or a crime scene per se. And there were no clues as to Wanda's whereabouts.

In a *Victoria Advocate* story published on August 29, 1979—the first anniversary of Wanda's disappearance—a reporter inquired about what investigators had in terms of leads, and Port Lavaca police officer Dana Whitten's response was succinct and to the point. "Nothing," he said. "Zero."

By then, Fred Priddy had divorced his missing wife and remarried, and he and the Port Lavaca community seemed to have moved on.

KATHRYN ELIZABETH COLLINS

On April 1, 1981, twenty-four-year-old Lolita resident Kathryn Collins disappeared in front of the Shell Fish restaurant just off the Port Lavaca causeway. A tire on her brown 1974 Chevrolet Caprice had gone flat, and she was attempting to change it, but she had no jack. A couple stopped to help and then left to borrow a jack. Then, a man in a tan van pulled up. Multiple witnesses saw the van and a man apparently offering to help Kathryn around 8:45 a.m., but the Caprice never moved, the tire was never replaced or repaired, and Kathryn vanished.

Kathryn had left her three-year-old son, Josh, with her boyfriend's parents and was headed into town for a doctor's appointment and to buy groceries. Her boyfriend's sister, Lucy Covarrubiaz, suspected foul play. "She wouldn't leave her son like that," Covarrubiaz insisted. "She just wasn't that kind of person."

WANDA PRIDDY WENT MISSING, and Kathryn Collins vanished. Then, like the story of the disappearance of Milton Sims, interest in these two young women's fates waned quickly.

Newspaper reports indicate that investigators eventually interviewed a suspect who was on parole for a sexual assault conviction and might have known both women, but detectives had no hard evidence that he was behind the disappearances. And the suspect died in North Texas in June 1991.

In December 1984, convicted serial killer Henry Lee Lucas[70] was interviewed in Victoria regarding a number of unsolved murders and missing persons cases in Victoria County, Calhoun County and the surrounding counties. But the dates he said he was in the area didn't correspond with the disappearances of Wanda Priddy or Kathryn Collins. In August 1991, investigators wondered if convicted serial killer Donald Leroy Evans[71] had been involved in the Port Lavaca disappearances, but no connection was ever established. Both Lucas and Evans claimed to have killed over three hundred people, but authorities officially linked them with only three each.

Kathryn Collins's son, Josh, went to live with his grandparents in Austin.

On April 25, 2002, Wanda and Kathryn were honored during a candlelight vigil, along with fifty-three Calhoun County victims of violent crime. On April 12, 2003, they were again honored with the fifty-three

Calhoun County victims of violent crime in conjunction with National Crime Victims' Rights Week.[72] The event was held at the Calhoun County Courthouse annex grounds.

April 1, 2021, marked the fortieth anniversary of Collins's disappearance, and August 29 will be the forty-third anniversary of Priddy's disappearance.

16

"WOOLLY" BULLY

The late spring and early summer of 1965 was a time of signs and wonders. News cycles were slower then, and headlines had time to hang around and play out. They got chewed on and mulled over before the next big newsbreak arrived.

The month of June started out particularly intriguing for Texans, but they didn't know it. On June 5, Domingo "Sam" Samudio, an unlikely star from Dallas, had a huge smash hit climb to number two on the Billboard Hot 100 chart, topped only by the Beach Boys' "Help Me, Rhonda." Samudio's band was called Sam the Sham and the Pharaohs, and the song was "Woolly Bully."

Staring up and no doubt scratching their heads were the Supremes with "Back in My Arms Again" at number three, Elvis Presley (and the Jordanaires) with "Crying in the Chapel" at number four, the Beatles with "Ticket to Ride" at five, the Four Tops with "I Can't Help Myself (Sugar Pie Honey Bunch)" at seven and "It's Not Unusual" by Tom Jones at ten. They were all established, legendary acts that enjoyed massive popularity, and they were suddenly vying for radio time with a Hispanic man from Dallas whose band fashion was faux Egyptian and whose hit started with a wacked-out Tex-Mex cadence: "uno, dos, one, two, tres, quatro."

Then, things got really strange.

On June 8, the United Soviet Socialist Republic launched Luna 6, an unmanned spacecraft that was intended to perform a landing on the moon. Due to the failure of a mid-course correction maneuver, however, Luna 6

Dallas band Sam the Sham and the Pharaohs reached number two in the Billboard Hot 100 charts in 1965 with a song called "Woolly Bully." It set the tone for the month of June that year. *Wikipedia Commons*.

failed to land, missing the moon by almost one hundred thousand miles. On June 12, an oddball couple named Sonny and Cher made their first television appearance on Dick Clark's American Bandstand. On June 14, Cincinnati Reds hurler Jim Maloney struck out eighteen New York Mets batters in a row—a nine-inning no hitter[73]—but his team failed to score and lost 1-0 in the eleventh inning after a Mets home run.

A week or so later, Houston resident Marvin Martin began trying to reach his elderly aunt and uncle, Edwina and Frederick Rogers. He called repeatedly and got no answer. When he went by their house at 1815 Driscoll Street (in the Montrose neighborhood) and knocked and still didn't get a response, he called the police. On the evening of June 23, Houston police officers Charles Bullock and L.M. Barta went by to make sure they were OK.

The front gate was padlocked, and the front door was locked. The back door was unlocked, but someone had stacked flowerpots and other household items against it, so it was difficult to open. After Bullock and Barta forced their way in, the place appeared to be empty. They performed a search anyway. Barta took the upstairs, and Bullock perused the downstairs and kitchen. They found no evidence that anybody was in the house until Bullock checked the refrigerator.

Examining a resident's refrigerator on a welfare check wasn't customary. "I don't know why I opened the refrigerator," Bullock said later. "For some reason I just opened it."

The refrigerator was chock-full of neatly stacked meat—which Bullock assumed was pork—and he observed that it would be a shame if it spoiled before Edwina and Frederick returned. But when he went to close the refrigerator door, something caught his eye.

Actually, it was another eye that caught his eye.

Another pair of eyes. And they were staring at him from a vegetable drawer.

He slammed the refrigerator door and gathered himself.

He opened the refrigerator door again, and the eyes still stared from seventy-nine-year-old Edwina Rogers's head. And she wasn't alone. Her eighty-one-year-old husband's head was in another crisper—but his eyes had been gouged out.

Bullock and Barta left the house in a hurry and relayed the details to homicide investigators.

THE GRUESOME SCENE GOT worse and then bizarre.

The "meat" in the refrigerator proved to be the remains of Edwina and Frederick Rogers. Their bodies had been drained of blood and dismembered in an upstairs bathroom. Their entrails had been flushed down a toilet and were discovered in a sewer a few blocks away.

Edwina Rogers had been beaten and shot in the head, execution style. Horrible, but a mild mercy. Frederick was dispatched by vicious claw hammer blows to the head, and his genitalia had been removed along with his eyeballs. The coroner's report indicated that the murders had been committed on June 20, 1965—Father's Day.

When authorities spoke with the nephew, Martin, the chief and only suspect was Charles Frederick Rogers, the forty-three-year-old son of the mutilated couple. He was nowhere to be found, but none of the neighbors even knew he had lived there to begin with. And not only did he live there, but he also owned the house.

Weirder still, even though they inhabited the same house, Charles Rogers was apparently a stranger to his parents. He was a peculiar recluse. He

Charles Frederick Rogers's parents were found chopped up in their refrigerator in Houston on June 23, 1965. *Courtesy of* Houston Chronicle.

cooked his meals on a hotplate in his attic bedroom. If he needed something from Edwina or Fred, he slipped notes under their bedroom door. A family maid later said that she wasn't sure if Charles had spoken to his mother face-to-face in years. And the neighbors weren't aware of his existence because if he left 1815 Driscoll, he did so before dawn and wouldn't return until after dark. "He was like a morning fog," Martin said. "He just faded in and out. He was a complete hermit."

When the United States got involved in World War II, Charles enlisted in the navy.[74] After the war, he earned a bachelor's degree in nuclear physics from the University of Houston and then became a seismologist. He worked for Shell Oil in places like Alaska and Canada for nine years. He held a commercial pilot's license, spoke several languages, played the violin and saxophone and was a ham radio enthusiast. At the time of his parents' murder, authorities couldn't establish whether Charles was gainfully employed or not. For his parents and his family, "Charles was simply an enigma, a gentle eccentric who chose to shun the world."[75]

The Houston Police Department had different ideas. Investigators believed Rogers was more like a wolf in sheep's clothing. Authorities suggested that Charles had turned into a coldblooded, methodical butcher who, after slaying his parents, meticulously carved up their bodies, carefully arranged them in the refrigerator and then spent at least twenty-four hours scrubbing the crime scene. Investigators found traces of blood in the upstairs bathroom and the attic bedroom. The claw hammer was also discovered in the attic bedroom, but there was no gun on the premises.

Police lieutenant Frank Crittenden, who led the Houston homicide division at the time of the murder, believed Rogers committed the crime while temporarily "mentally unbalanced." Detective James Paulk, who also worked on the case at that time, did not concur. "It took a lot of time to clean up all that blood," he said, "and I think he did it to give himself more time to get as far away as possible."

The Houston Police Department issued an all-points bulletin and initiated a nationwide manhunt, but Charles had simply vanished. The gruesome

Charles Frederick Rogers's father and mother, Fred and Edwina. *Courtesy of* Houston Chronicle.

double homicide soon became known as the Icebox Murders. And a summer that had started strange, got scary and became macabre, ended even darker. On July 28, 1965, President Lyndon Baines Johnson authorized the first official use of U.S ground combat forces in Vietnam.

CHARLES ROGERS WAS DECLARED dead in absentia in July 1975 to probate the Rogers' estate. In the years that followed, a fantastical mythology sprang up around the case and the chief suspect. As Jake Rossen put it in "Cold Case: Revisiting Houston's Infamous Icebox Murders" in the November 4, 2019 edition of *Mental Floss* magazine, conspiracy theorists began "using the blank canvas of the crime scene to try and attach deeper meaning to Charles' life." In *The Man on the Grassy Knoll* (1992), John R. Craig and Philip A. Rogers claimed that Charles had actually been part of a three-man CIA hit team (posing as tramps) that assassinated President John F. Kennedy in Dallas in 1963 and that he must have been compelled to murder his parents when they discovered damning evidence of his involvement. Other conspiracy theorists claim Charles was also a handler in James Earl Ray's assassination of Martin Luther King Jr. in Memphis in 1968.

Some people believe Charles Frederick Rogers was involved in the assassination of John F. Kennedy two years earlier. *Wikimedia Commons*.

In *The Icebox Murders* (2003), forensic accountants Hugh and Martha Gardenier argued that Edwina and Frederick (who was a retired real estate agent) had been abusive parents and "devious con artists" and that Charles slew them in an "orgy of violence" because they had taken advantage of him financially, taking out loans against the house he owned and forging his signature on deeds to other properties Charles owned so they could sell them.

The general consensus that evolved held that parts of *The Man on the Grassy Knoll* were pure speculation if not fantasy, and *The Icebox Murders*, while less fantastical, was a work of "fact-based fiction and supposition."

Regardless of whether or not the tabloid hijack of Charles Frederick Rogers's education and personal history holds up to serious scrutiny or the exact details of his disappearance are ever established, one thing seems obvious. Rogers—a possibly brilliant but twisted outlier—sought and achieved oblivion voluntarily.

17

FATE OF THE *SAN ANTONIO*

T he second Texas Navy was a scrappy, redheaded stepchild. It was fierce but woefully underfunded. The fleet leadership was capable and driven, but its civilian overseers were feckless and deceitful. The Republic of Texas couldn't afford the second navy to begin with, and once the schooners it employed were seaborne, the republic couldn't raise funds to keep them outfitted or maintained, much less pay the sailors who operated the fleet. In fact, the short run of the second Texas Navy is perhaps the most indisputable evidence that the Republic of Texas was a banana republic.

The Texas Navy was created in January 1836, with the procurement of four schooners: *Invincible, Brutus, Independence* and *Liberty*. Led by Commodore Charles Hawkins, these vessels helped ensure Texas independence by thwarting a Mexican blockade of the Texas coast, seizing ships carrying reinforcements and supplies to the Mexican army and rerouting those provisions to supply Texas soldiers. But even after General Antonio López de Santa Anna was defeated at the Battle of San Jacinto on April 21, 1836, and signed the Treaties of Velasco (Velasco is now known as Surfside Beach) on May 14, 1836—ceasing hostilities and marking the first steps toward the official recognition of Texas autonomy—Mexico refused to acknowledge Texas independence. And by mid-1837, the *Invincible, Brutus, Independence* and *Liberty* had all been captured, sold, run aground or lost at sea.

Late in 1838, Mirabeau B. Lamar, the second president of the Republic of Texas, commissioned the second Texas Navy. He believed the fledgling nation was still vulnerable to Mexican invasion and felt that the republic's attempts to court allies and support from Europe would be more successful if Texas could defend itself. Commodore Edwin Ward Moore, an Alexandria Academy graduate and a fourteen-year veteran of the U.S. Navy, was named commander of the second Texas Navy, and President Lamar purchased six new warships from Frederick Dawson, an elite shipbuilder in Baltimore, for $280,000. The ships of the new fleet, which included the 600-ton ship of war *Austin*, the 170-ton schooner *San Bernard*, the 170-ton schooner *San Antonio*, the 170-ton schooner *San Jacinto* and the 400-ton brig *Wharton*, arrived intermittently from 1839 to 1840.

Under Lamar, the Texas Navy policed the Gulf of Mexico effectively for a while, but the fledgling Republic exhausted its financial resources, and this led to severe economic difficulties. In fact, Dawson didn't receive final payment for the ships he built for Texas until well after American statehood was achieved.

When a revolt started in the Yucatán, President Lamar sent Commodore Moore to exploit the situation. Moore set sail in command of the *Austin* and complemented by the *San Bernard* and the *San Antonio*.

After a long lull in hostilities between Mexico and Texas, however, the republic's congress cut naval appropriations. Every vessel of the Texas Navy was decommissioned except the *San Antonio* and the *San Bernard*, and they spent May to October 1841 surveying the Texas coastline. Contemporary maps of the republic's ports and harbors were often wildly inaccurate, and this made private and commercial passage hazardous.

On September 18, 1841, an alliance was struck between Texas and the Yucatán, the latter pledging to pay Texas $8,000 a month for the upkeep of the Texas fleet if it defended the province's interests. President Lamar approved this arrangement and ordered the fleet to leave for Yucatán. On December 13, 1841, Moore departed Galveston for Yucatán once more, again commanding the *Austin* and flanked by the *San Bernard* and the *San Antonio*. Sam Houston subsequently succeeded Lamar as president and immediately ordered Commodore Moore's small fleet to return.

President Houston's orders did not reach Commodore Moore until the spring of 1842, and Moore returned to Texas in May. The Yucatecans were having no problems with Mexico at the time, so they suspended the upkeep agreement with Texas until such time as the navy was needed again.

In the meantime, the *San Antonio* had been ordered to New Orleans for refitting. Maintenance was slow going, however, because ship outfitters in New Orleans were no longer accepting Texas credit, and President Houston had authorized no funds for repairs, provisions or replacements for the depleted crew. Then, on February 11, 1842, as the *San Antonio* sat anchored in the Mississippi River across from New Orleans, a mutiny occurred.

After the principal officers had gone ashore, several members of the crew procured liquor and became inebriated. A drunken marine sergeant unsteadily petitioned the deck officer for permission to go ashore, and the officer informed the marine sergeant that none of the officers remaining on board had the authority to grant them leave. The discussion became heated, and Lieutenant Charles Fuller emerged from the galley to inquire about the disturbance. When crew members reiterated their request to go ashore, the lieutenant instructed the ship's guard to arm themselves. Lieutenant Fuller escaped a tomahawk attack, only to be laid low by a gunshot. The mutineers locked the other officers in a cabin and went ashore.

The mutineers were captured quickly and imprisoned in New Orleans. A mutineer named Seymour Oswald escaped, and another, Benjamin Pompilly, died in prison while awaiting trial. Pompilly reportedly confessed to Lieutenant Fuller's murder on his deathbed.

Presidents Houston and Lamar had both previously sought Mexico's recognition of Texas as a sovereign nation, but by mid-1842, President Houston was sabotaging every attempt to convince Mexico to acknowledge the republic's independence because he was trying to get the United States to annex Texas, and peril played better for his allies in Washington, D.C. Houston thereby refused to release any appropriations the congress earmarked for the navy.

With his fleet literally falling apart, Commodore Moore publicly supported President Houston but privately fumed. He dispatched the *San Antonio* to Yucatán to ask that their naval agreement be reinstated and their $8,000 monthly subsidy for maintenance be restored, but the *San Antonio* never made it. The ship disappeared in the Gulf of Mexico during a storm in September 1842, taking the entire crew—including many of those scheduled to testify against the mutineers—with it.

Mutineer Joseph D. Shepherd, however, had turned state's evidence to gain a pardon, and after the *San Antonio* vanished, Shepherd was the court-martial prosecution's chief witness. On April 22, 1843, one of the mutineers received one hundred lashes. On April 26, four additional *San Antonio* mutineers were hanged at the *Austin*'s yardarm and then relegated to the same watery grave their shipmates on the *San Antonio* were consigned to seven months before. Shepherd received his pardon but perished three weeks later during a naval confrontation with Mexican vessels.

United States president James K. Polk signed a bill annexing the foundering Republic of Texas on December 29, 1845. Texas was formally added as the twenty-eighth state of the Union on February 19, 1846. The unsettled dispute over the border between Texas and Mexico caused relations between the United States and Mexico to deteriorate almost immediately, and the Mexican-American War began only a few months later.

The wreck of the *San Antonio* has never been located.

18

EUCLID'S GETAWAY

After Euclid Taylor Fant Jr. had been missing for five weeks, his family prevailed upon *Time* magazine to publish a personal appeal. The Fant family controlled the Gladiola Mills flour empire in Sherman, Texas, and forty-one-year-old Euclid was an avid reader of the periodical. The appeal appeared in the November 3, 1958 edition of *Time*: "Euclid—there is no problem as great as this mutual grief. There is no problem we can't face and solve in love together. Only tragedy and sorrow are possible without you here. We love you and need you desperately. Please contact Bobbie or Arch or me at once—Jim."

James A. "Jim" Fant was Euclid's sixty-year-old brother and the president of the Gladiola Mills operation. Barbara K. "Bobbie" Fant was Euclid's wife.

Curiously, however, the law enforcement agencies participating in the investigation of Fant's disappearance were still operating under the assumption that he was the victim of foul play or had an accident and suffered amnesia. The Fant family's appeal in *Time* wasn't addressed to an assailant or kidnapper, nor did the Fant family receive ransom requests. The appeal in *Time* also doesn't ask any potential good Samaritans who might have stumbled across Fant and helped him to come forward with information. The Fant family's communiqué basically addresses Euclid as if he had disappeared of his own accord.

On September 24, 1958, Euclid told his wife that he was going to Dallas on business and that he'd be home by dinner. He cashed a check for $150 at the Grayson Hotel in Sherman, visited the offices of the Sherman United Fund (where he served as the advance solicitation chairman) and then vanished.

A father of three, Fant was an economics lecturer at Austin College and a part-time insurance agent for the Pilot Life Insurance Company. Referred to as a civic leader in contemporary reports, Euclid was also the former local Rotary Club president and district governor. He had expensive tastes in food and clothing, and his hobby was golf. Though purported to be something of an economic genius, he was a low-level executive for the Gladiola Mills organization, and his older brother appeared to steer him clear of a prominent hand in the family business. Euclid dabbled at this and that, but apparently did so at an almost constant financial loss.

On Saturday, September 27, Bobbie Fant said that her husband sometimes picked up hitchhikers, and she was afraid he might have been kidnapped or attacked and that he might be suffering from amnesia. She claimed that everything had been fine before he left. "He didn't act unusual in any way," she said. But Euclid's brother Jim disagreed. He said he could tell that Euclid was worried about something. Jack Barrett, a businessman who saw Euclid that morning, supported Jim Fant's opinion. He described Euclid as being "in a rather pensive mood."

Though Euclid was an "enthusiastic" air traveler and abhorred railroad passage, his car, a 1955 Plymouth sedan, turned up in a parking lot at the Union Terminal train station in Dallas on the morning of Sunday, September 29. At first glance, nothing seemed amiss. The car windows were secure, the handbrake was "firmly set" (which was Euclid's habit) and the Dallas Police found an open copy of the *Wall Street Journal* newspaper dated September 24 in the front seat. But one of the front fenders was damaged, the key was still in the ignition, the gas tank was empty and, underneath the newspaper, authorities identified blood spatters on the seat and a book. The search also yielded Euclid's eyeglasses and his wallet, which still had his identification information in it but no money.

The discovery heightened concerns that Euclid had met with foul play, but when Dallas homicide detective Will Fritz set up an appointment with Bobbie Fant at the Police and Courts Building in Dallas on Wednesday, October 1, she failed to show. When reporters questioned Mrs. Fant about missing her scheduled conversation with Detective Fritz, she denied that she had agreed to the appointment and then clammed up, abruptly ending the interview.

MISSING PERSON
Euclid Taylor Fant

Seeking information as to whereabouts of person whose picture and description listed below.

MISSING from Sherman, Texas

Since September 24, 1958

Please pass this information on to your local newspaper and radio-TV Station.

DESCRIPTION:

Age 41; Height 5 ft. 8in.; Wt. 145 lbs. Gray hair parted on left side. Blue eyes, ruddy complexion, crooked teeth; always wears glasses; clean shaven, wears gold band wedding ring; Occupation: Life Insurance Underwriter; part time educator at Austin College, Sherman, Texas. Closely associated with Presbyterian Church. Active in Rotary Club; Past District Governor of District 188. Previous occupations: Automobile agency owner, radio station owner, hobby, golf; married 15 years and is the father of 3 children, Beverly age 13, Johnny age 11, and Bob age 6. Wife's name is Barbara.

Possibly an Amnesia case.

If you are in possession of any information regarding the whereabouts of the above, please communicate with the undersigned.

Notify Mrs. Barbara Fant, Sherman, Texas, or Sheriff Woody Blanton, Sheriff of Grayson County, Texas, Sherman, Texas, or Police Chief Les Tribble, Sherman, Texas.

Missing person flyer for Euclid Taylor Fant. *Courtesy of the UNT Digital Library.*

On Saturday, October 4, 1958, a forty-year-old Fort Worth man was taken into custody in Dallas for a lie detector test after bragging about knowing what happened to Fant at a Mansfield Highway tavern the previous day. The incident produced no leads.

On Thursday, October 16, Grayson County sheriff T.W. Blanton announced that a former pastor, Reverend James Bullock (then a resident of Tennessee), had come forward and claimed he ran into Euclid Fant in a Times Square theater lobby in New York City the day Euclid's car was found in Dallas. According to the *Dallas Morning News*, when Reverend Bullock greeted the individual he assumed to be Euclid, "the man excused himself and walked away." The man's exit failed to temper Bullock's belief that the person in question was actually his friend from Sherman, and he relayed news of Euclid's sighting to James Fant.

THE FANT FAMILY'S *TIME* magazine appeal received no responses.

By February 1959, Dallas investigators were considering a twenty-six-year-old Black man who had hurled a White rape victim out of a nineteenth-

Texas Ranger Lewis C. Rigler worked the Virginia Carpenter and Euclid T. Fant disappearances. *Courtesy of the* Fort Worth Star-Telegram.

floor window of the Adolphus Hotel as a person of interest, but nothing linked him to Euclid. On Thursday, August 13, 1959, Bobbie Fant was granted control of her and her husband's property and affairs by the fifteenth district court in Sherman. Euclid's mother, Lily Fant, died in January 1960, and on April 14 of that year, her estate willed Euclid $143,215.[76]

Euclid never appeared to claim his inheritance, and the money was eventually used to pay his debts and provide funds for Bobbie and their three children.

In the summer of 1962, a man thought to be Euclid Fant was picked up by New York City police officers and taken to Bellevue Hospital. The Fant family sent identifying photos and notes, but the report turned out to be a mistake.

Though it was not splashed across news reports at the time, the Sherman and Dallas Police Departments' attempts to establish what happened to Euclid Fant Jr. were soon supplemented by the efforts of the Texas Rangers and the FBI. In the end, they were all unsuccessful, but Lewis Rigler, the lead Ranger in the search for Fant, later wrote a book that touched on some aspects of the case. In his *In the Line of Duty: Reflections of a Texas Ranger Private* (originally published in 1984), some interesting details emerged. First, on Friday, September 26—the day before Bobbie Fant said she was afraid Euclid might have been kidnapped or attacked and that everything had been fine before he left, she told investigators that if her husband was alive, she felt that he was "sick" and "that something just snapped." Second, Euclid had recently but unsuccessfully attempted to secure a $10,000 loan from his brother Jim, his doctor, his pastor and several other people. Third, the blood spatter discovered on the front seat of Euclid's Plymouth had not been small, and, though a copy of the *Wall Street Journal* had covered it, the newspaper itself had picked up no traces of the blood, meaning that the blood had dried before the newspaper had been used to conceal it.

Rigler also wrote that a lead Bobbie Fant mentioned eventually provided some background:

> *Mrs. Fant remembered that before Euclid's disappearance he had periodically received telephone calls beginning in late 1955, from a man named John Joseph Daly. The calls came from Norwalk, Connecticut, and various places throughout the U.S. When Mrs. Fant questioned her husband about the calls, he was rather vague and indefinite as to the nature of the acquaintance. Since Euclid's disappearance, Mrs. Fant had received several telephone calls from Beverly Hills, California, from the same man she believed, always asking for Euclid. In December, after Euclid Fant had been missing for almost three months, he received a Christmas card at his post office box signed "John Joseph Daly," with the return address of 100 Lexington Avenue, Norwalk, Connecticut, and the notation, "Please drop me a card."*

The Norwalk Police Department was contacted about Daly, and his extensive record included arrests for breaking and entering, theft, vagrancy and sodomy. Rigler and members of other law enforcement agencies cast a wide net for Daly but had little luck. In June 1959, Daly walked into the Port Arthur Police Department and asked to be arrested, because he was penniless and had no place to go. When authorities involved with the Fant case interviewed Daly there, he admitted to meeting Fant in 1955 and beginning a brief homosexual relationship with him. Daly also said that during their relationship, Fant had set him up in an apartment, sent him money and helped him find jobs.

Rigler wrote that Euclid Taylor Fant Jr.'s disappearance was the "top case" in North Texas for a few years, but with little evidence, no new clues and Fant's own family wondering if he hadn't vanished of his own accord, the case dropped out of the newspapers and became a low priority for regional law enforcement agencies.

Rigler passed away on June 25, 2009, after a lengthy battle with cancer. Well into the 1980s, Fant's children were still contacting him from time to time to find out if there were any new developments in their father's case, but Rigler had no news. When Rigler was interviewed in 1994 by Robert Nieman, a staff member of the Texas Ranger Hall of Fame and Museum, he lamented never finding Euclid Fant but also expressed sympathy. "Well, my opinion is, he wanted to get away and disappear," Rigler said. "That's my opinion, and maybe I'm wrong. But I believe that."

To say that homosexuality was frowned upon in the 1950s is a preposterous understatement, and if Euclid T. Fant Jr. was engaging in a homosexual relationship with Daly (and possibly others), his existential desperation must have been intense and unceasing. If Rigler was right, Fant might have used his "economic genius" for the long game, setting funds aside all along or siphoning funds that made his business ventures run at a perpetual loss. Then, when and if he made his escape, he wouldn't need anything from his family. His wife could simply take over the estate and collect his inheritance.

Was Euclid T. Fant a victim of foul play or, like Charles Frederick Rogers, a brilliant outlier who voluntarily relegated himself to oblivion?

19

MOFFAT MYSTERY

O n Saturday, April 13, 1985, the Bell County Historical Commission placed and dedicated Texas State Historical Marker no. 3431, devoted to the small, unincorporated community of Moffat. The state of Texas now boasts over sixteen thousand markers, but the Moffat historical marker is unique. It concedes a blatant civic error, introduces a mystery and might allege a crime. And the civic error might have been a purposeful response related to the crime. The marker states:

> *Founded in 1857 by New York native Dr. Chauncy W. Moffet and his wife, Amelia, the town of Moffat came to be known by a misspelling of their name. A Union loyalist during the Civil War, Dr. Moffet was impressed into Confederate service, but later also served the Union. He disappeared mysteriously after returning to the Moffat community in 1868. The town was platted that year by D.F. and Calista Wiswell. Moffat soon had 3 churches, a school, a post office, stores, and small industries. The Moffat Cemetery, begun before the Civil War, is still in use.*

To be a Union loyalist in Texas leading up to the Civil War was a dangerous prospect. On August 10, 1862, thirty-four German immigrants camped along the Nueces River were slaughtered by Confederate troops for attempting to escape conscription by fleeing to Mexico.[77] Two months later, forty-two more suspected Union loyalists were executed in the Great Hanging in Gainesville. Dr. Chauncey W. Moffet was a Union loyalist *impressed* into serving the Confederacy (possibly as a surgeon). He was forcibly inspired to reconsider his moral and political reservations so that he might march alongside his Bell County neighbors.

As the Moffat historical marker nonchalantly states, Moffet "later also served the Union." In other words, his coerced Confederate conscription didn't stick, and he joined the Union, possibly serving until the end of the Civil War. Then, presumably, he was reluctant to return to Moffat, due to his Union service.

According to the marker, he didn't return to the town bearing his misspelled surname until 1868—probably prudently remaining absent to allow the dust to settle. The marker, however, suggests that he didn't wait long enough.

By then, Texans were embittered by Reconstruction and lurching en masse to embrace the lost cause ideology that defined the American South for the next century. Many of Moffet's former Moffat neighbors would have viewed him with open contempt and undisguised hostility—it's no wonder he subsequently went missing.

In *Bloody Bell County: Vignettes of Violence and Mayhem in Central Texas* (2011), Rick Miller notes that "the years in Bell County immediately following the Civil War were filled with uncontrolled violence and were probably the most violent period in the county's history" and that "many murders went unrecorded." Before the war, the citizens of Bell County had been staunch supporters of Sam Houston, who was then governor and a bold, vociferously

The Great Hanging of Union sympathizers in Gainesville, Texas, in October 1862. *From* Frank Leslie's Illustrated Newspaper *(February 20, 1864).*

anti-secessionist force in Texas politics. But Bell County was quickly caught up in the secessionist fervor, and when Houston's governorship was vacated after he refused to take an oath of allegiance to the Confederate States of America, most folks didn't seem to care.

According to George W. Tyler's *The History of Bell County*, the White population of the county when the war started was approximately four thousand, "yet the muster rolls of her soldiery credited her with more than one thousand men and boys who donned the Confederate gray." Tyler proudly noted that "no county or country, we believe, ever made a better showing of loyalty to home and fireside." But fervors fade. Bell County saw its share of Confederate deserters who roamed the cedar brakes and outskirts of the major towns and no doubt heard reports of neighbors—like Dr. Moffet—who broke with the cause and joined the other side. And the general negative opinion of and animosity toward these "traitors" did not abate after the guns grew silent. In fact, it only got worse. Tyler blamed it on the Texas Unionists themselves:

> *Behind these and other acts of violence and outrage, too numerous to chronicle here, there stood the vengeful shadow and threatening attitude of certain citizens of Bell County, who had opposed secession and had sulkily bided the termination of the war. When the Confederacy finally went down, they promptly sought and obtained places of official authority and power under the military arm of the Federal government, and in revenge for past injuries, real or fancied, used their official influence to bring about the arrests of these citizens and of many others under trumped up charges of disloyalty to the United States.*

Moffet, of course, hadn't been one of these zealots. A Yankee, perhaps, but a carpetbagger,[78] no.

Tellingly, however, Tyler's *History of Bell County* also lauds the Ku Klux Klan, claiming its members "accomplished great work and in an orderly way…[and] if there was the occasional act of physical violence, someone else forced the issue and the event."

Regardless of who or which side was most aggrieved, Texans who were sympathetic to the Union were often murdered. And in one case, Hiram Christian, a county judge who Tyler claimed was "the leader of the scalawag and negrophile element in Bell County," was apparently tracked down after he left the bench in Bell County around 1866 and was assassinated in Springfield, Missouri, on Friday, May 24, 1867.

SOME ACCOUNTS INDICATED THAT Moffet came back to Moffat to settle his affairs, "sell his holdings and claim his livestock." Moffet's wife, Amelia, had relocated to Illinois during the Civil War, probably before or just after her husband switched sides. She remained in Illinois when Moffet returned, and there is no indication she ever saw him again.[79]

According to *A Standard History of Kansas and Kansans* (1918)[80] by William Elsey Connelley:

> *Dr. Chauncey* [sic] *Moffet was a capable physician and was the pioneer in that profession at his locality in Texas. He was a northern man settled in a hotbed of pro-slavery sentiments, and though living in the midst of political and radical enemies he showed a complete lack of fear and an absolute contempt for all the bitterness and hostility aroused against him. Though he owned slaves himself, he kept them only long enough to teach them to read and then freed them and started them north to liberty. He freed all his slaves at the outbreak of the war, and this act opened the breach between him and his fellow citizens beyond all possibility of healing. In fact it brought on an open war upon him and was followed by many personal encounters and ultimately led to his death. He attended the meeting of some forty Texas settlers at the opening of the war and shortly after he had freed his own slaves. This meeting was called for the consideration of matters relating to the state of the community. One of the pro-slavery men, not then acquainted with Doctor Moffet, referred to the latter's act in liberating his slaves in such a tirade of abuse as to arouse all the indignation of which Doctor Moffet was capable. Notwithstanding the fact that every man in the room, except a Mr. Kirkendall, was his personal and political enemy, Doctor Moffet seized the heavy glass in front of him, and from which he had been drinking buttermilk, threw it across the table at his antagonist and struck him full in the face, knocking him out of his chair. Jumping to his feet he then grabbed the pitcher of buttermilk, not yet empty, and poured the contents into the face of the victim as he lay on the floor. This sudden outbreak served to line up the participants of the meeting each according to his political sentiments and belief, pistols were drawn and a battle opened which, as it appeared to Mr. Kirkendall, the only friend the Doctor had in the house, could surely end only in the killing of this fearless and combative Unionist. But with a pistol and his knife Doctor Moffet shot and carved his way out of the room, leaped over an eight-foot board fence in the yard while fifty shots were sent after him, reaching his horse and made his escape. Two days afterward he made himself known to his friend Kirkendall under*

the latter's corncrib, asked for ammunition and provision and made his way out of the locality. Soon after the incident his wife gathered some of their horses and drove back north, the Confederates confiscating all the balance of the family property. Doctor Moffet was then forced into the service of the Confederate side and was enrolled as a surgeon. He finally made his escape from the Southern army, deserting at Fort Smith, Arkansas, and joining an Iowa company and regiment. Toward the close of the war he returned to Moffet, Texas, and there his stormy career came to an end. The old hostility which had been aroused in the early part of the war still followed him, and a large number of Southerners finally gathered and made open war upon him. Again he proved an adept in self-defense, but was killed a short time afterward by a pretended friend near Fairfield, Texas. After his death his body was examined and was found to be marked by fourteen scars, wounds made by knife or bullet in the many encounters he had had with his enemies.

This account probably approaches a comic book version of the actual events in Dr. Moffet's life but might be useful in terms of cross-reference. Some Moffet family genealogy research indicates that Dr. Moffet died in 1872 at the age of forty-seven in Texas. According to the *Story of Bell County, Texas* (1988), compiled by E.A. Limmer and the Bell County Historical Commission, Dr. Moffet was murdered in 1874 while trying to drive his livestock north. This timeline certainly would not have made his killing at the hand of Bell County vigilantes farfetched. As late as June of that year, a Bell County posse stormed the Belton jail and slaughtered nine prisoners in cold blood.[81]

At this juncture, Tyler's *History of Bell County* might sum matters up best: "The military and reconstruction period, succeeding the War between the States, brought along its train of evils in our county as it did everywhere throughout the South. And these conditions are difficult, if not impossible, to fairly and fully describe from memory or tradition, after the long lapse of years and the sensitive silence which has brooded over the deplorable events."

Did it take Moffet four to six years to settle his affairs and ready his herd for the northward journey? Did he change his name and relocate and resettle temporarily in Texas before heading north? Did vigilantes from Bell County track him down in Fairfield or somewhere else?

Connelley's *Standard History of Kansas and Kansans* account of Dr. Moffet mentions Moffet's friend Kirkendall, but this is probably a misspelling. In a section titled "New Communities and Settlers in the Fifties" (as in the 1850s),

Tyler's *History of Bell County* states that "from 1852 to 1855, the country about Cedar Creek, Owl Creek, and on the Stampede Creek began to settle up." Of the men who relocated to that area (a section of which would later become Moffat) from other states or other sections of Texas were Abner Kuykendall (who fought in the Texas Revolution), Hiram Christian and Dr. C.W. Moffet. And today, Moffat Road off State Hwy 36 is intersected by Kuykendall Mountain Road, which used to run toward a community called Aiken. Kuykendall built a flour mill and steam saw in Aiken in 1857, the same year Moffat was supposedly founded by Dr. Moffet.

Lake Belton was impounded in 1954, and Aiken now rests under its waters. Kuykendall moved to Johnson County after the Civil War and died five and a half months after Christian, on November 9, 1867. His final resting place is the Oakland Cemetery in Grandview, Texas. Christian is reportedly buried in Greene County near Springfield, Missouri. The site of Dr. Moffet's death and the location of his grave are both unknown, but natives of the town named after him seem to have observed an interesting, perhaps unconscious, intermittent tug-of-war regarding the erroneous nomenclature of the community well into the twentieth century.

According to a medical journal obituary for Dr. James H. Haley, MD, he moved to the Bell County town of *Moffett*, Texas, in the autumn of 1873, "where he lived to the hour of his death" on February 20, 1887.[82] And when Mrs. Hattie Grimes passed away near San Saba on July 29, 1939, her obituary noted that she had been a native of *Moffet*, Texas, and that she had been born there on February 21, 1871.[83] It seems that, for a time at least, Moffat was known by its correct spelling (or something closer to it) by some or misspelled on purpose by others, perhaps as a latent act of defiance.

GILMER GIRL'S GHOST

T he State of Texas is no stranger to miscarriages of justice. The King Ranch disappearances of Luther and John Blanton and Reyes Ramirez and Jesus Rivera offer evidence of that. Fort Worth oilman Cullen Davis's acquittals for murder and the conspiracy to commit murder in the 1970s were a tabloid mockery of jurisprudence in the Lone Star State, as was the ludicrous conviction of former army veteran and Texas Tech student Timothy Brian Cole of rape in 1986.[84] More recent farcical shams of Texas justice include the June 2013 acquittal of thirty-year-old Ezekiel Gilbert, who got away with gunning down a twenty-three-year-old escort named Lenora Frago with an assault rifle in San Antonio on Christmas Eve in 2009, and the ten-year probation given to sixteen-year-old Burleson teenager Ethan Couch after he killed four people and injured nine (leaving one paralyzed for life) while driving under the influence of alcohol and drugs. His legal team mounted the now infamous "affluenza" defense,[85] claiming that Couch shouldn't be punished too severely for his crimes because his parents had neglected to teach him the concepts of responsibility and consequences.

The list goes on and on, but perhaps the most egregious example of a miscarriage of justice in the Lone Star state involved the disappearance of seventeen-year-old Kelly Dae Wilson in Gilmer on the evening of January 5, 1992.

Wilson closed the Northeast Texas Video store at 100 Buffalo Road with her manager, Joe Henry, at 8:30 p.m. and drove a half block to the Gilmer National Bank (at 215 North Titus) to make a deposit. Unbeknownst to her, a seventeen-year-old classmate named Michael Biby had slashed one of her tires. Wilson must not have noticed at first, and surveillance cameras at the bank recorded her making the deposit.

Kelly Dae Wilson was never seen or heard from again.

Her car was later found parked in front of the video store. The tire that had been slashed was completely off the wheel rim. Authorities assumed Wilson had driven back to the video store to get help or find a ride home.

Respected thirty-five-year-old Gilmer Police sergeant James York Brown was placed in charge of the investigation, and after an intensive three-day search for Kelly Wilson, he declared her disappearance a missing person case. But days, weeks and months went by, and no evidence of Wilson's whereabouts turned up. The Gilmer Police arrested Biby early on, but he was only charged with criminal mischief. He served a twenty-five-day sentence and was fined $500 for slashing Wilson's tire. He was never charged in connection with Wilson's disappearance or murder. The Gilmer Police then looked hard at Wilson's boyfriend, Christopher Michael Denton. Acquaintances said Denton had a bad temper, but he had an alibi. According to his first cousin Brent Ward, the two had been driving around together and hanging out that evening.

Not long after alibiing his cousin, Ward left the state to serve as a Mormon missionary in California. But he was called back to Gilmer and charged with two counts of perjury in June 1993. He had apparently lied about being in Denton's truck the night of Wilson's disappearance and tried to get a classmate Madi Cramer to give him an alibi. He was eventually cleared of the original perjury charges but then indicted again three months later.

On October 30, 1992—ten months after Kelly Wilson's disappearance—Christopher Denton stabbed someone and was charged with aggravated assault. He pled guilty to the charge on February 4, 1993, served 120 days in jail and began a ten-year probation sentence. Though he was the chief suspect in the Wilson case, authorities said the two cases were not connected.

Sergeant Brown spent hundreds of extra hours working on Wilson's case, but the Gilmer Police Department didn't get very far because it didn't have a body or a crime scene and local parties weren't talking. Brown also complained about a lack of cooperation among state law enforcement agencies. Desperate, Brown even allowed a psychic to offer tips regarding the investigation. They led nowhere.

On January 16, 1993, a little over a year after Kelly Wilson's disappearance, Michael Biby was reportedly abducted and beaten by two men. Biby said

MISSING
Kelly Wilson

Kelly Wilson is a white female, DOB 5/18/74. At the time of her disappearance she was 5'7" tall, weighed 120 pounds; she has blue eyes and light brown hair.

Kelly was last seen Sunday, January 5, 1992 in Gilmer (Upshur County), Texas. Foul play is suspected.

Anyone with information about Kelly Wilson's disappearance is asked to call Scott Lyford, special prosecutor for Upshur County. **PERSONS WITH IN-FORMATION ARE ASKED TO CALL, EVEN IF THEY HAVE GIVEN INFORMATION TO PREVIOUS INVESTIGATORS.** Anonymity is guaranteed. You will not be required to give your name.

1-800-657-5226
Scott Lyford, Special Prosecutor, Upshur County
Steve Baggs, Investigator   Brooks Fleig, Investigator

Missing persons ad for Kelly Rae Wilson. *Courtesy of* Longview News-Journal.

he was grabbed on a Gilmer street at about 1:20 a.m., stuffed into a car and taken to an unknown location in Upshur County. Then, the two men roughed him up and left him to walk back to town. The incident reportedly left Biby with a swollen ear, but Sergeant Brown was suspicious. "It's kind of unusual the way he is telling it," he said, declining to expand any further.

Biby moved out of state soon after.

ON THE NIGHT OF July 26, 1988, the body of seventeen-year-old Tate Rowland was discovered hanging from a horse apple tree on a backcountry road just outside of Childress, Texas, 370 miles west of Gilmer. His death was ruled a suicide, but lots of folks didn't buy it. They believed something more sinister was behind it.

Three years after Rowland's death, Terrie Trosper, Rowland's twenty-two-year-old sister, was found face down in her bed, dead. Her death was ruled an accident, but whispers began to swirl. Some folks held that Rowland had been killed by a satanic cult and that Trosper—who reportedly never believed that her brother had committed suicide—was murdered because she had uncovered too much about the cult. Panic soon gripped the community, and Childress's hysteria soon contributed to a frenzied, irrational cacophony that was sweeping across the nation. Skip Hollandsworth's piece in the July 1992 edition of *Texas Monthly* described it best:

> *Satan hunters had long insisted that deadly occult organizations were moving into the heartland of America, luring in youthful recruits with sex and drugs, the lyrics of heavy metal music, and fantasy games like Dungeons and Dragons. The threat, they said, could not be taken lightly. Indeed, most law enforcement agencies in the country were placing on their staffs a specialized "cult cop," an officer trained to spot satanic villainy. The Texas Department of Public Safety was sending local police departments a handout listing thirty ways to determine if someone had been killed as a result of an occult ritual. Cult awareness agencies were springing up to remind the public that today's candle-burning teenager might be tomorrow's baby killer.*

On May 5, 1993, three eight-year-old boys—Steve Branch, Christopher Byers and Michael Moore—were reported missing in West Memphis, Arkansas. On May 6, the bodies of the three second graders were discovered bludgeoned near a local creek. They had been stripped naked and hogtied with their own shoelaces. Autopsies revealed that Byers succumbed to multiple injuries, and Branch and Moore died of multiple injuries and drowning.

The horrific murders made national headlines, and by early June, three local teenagers—sixteen-year-old Charles Baldwin, eighteen-year-old Michael Wayne Echols and seventeen-year-old Jessie Lloyd Misskelley[86]— had been accused of murdering the young boys as part of a satanic ritual. The arrest and theory of the harrowing crime garnered even more headlines.

Meanwhile, two Gilmer area Child Protective Services workers, supervisor Deborah Minshew and Ann Goar, had been investigating the possibility of generational child molestation allegations against the extended Kerr family in rural Gilmer. During their investigation, they attended a cult crime seminar, and in a matter of time, they began to surmise that some of the testimony they witnessed in their sessions with the children—and one nine-year-old boy in particular—indicated the members of the Kerr family were involved in satanic rituals. And before

Some Gilmer residents were convinced that Kelly Wilson's disappearance was part of a satanic ritual. *Courtesy of the first printed edition of Dante's* Divine Comedy *(1491).*

these discussions were completed, they apparently included hints that these rituals were connected to the rape and murder of Kelly Wilson.

When the charges of child molestation were formally leveled, Upshur County prosecutor Tim Cone recused himself because he had represented members of the Kerr family when he was a defense attorney. Child Protective Services placed sixteen young children of the Kerr defendants in foster care, and the state appointed Galveston lawyer Scott Lyford as special prosecutor of the case. Lyford made Minshew and Goar part of his investigative team and brought in self-described occult expert Brooks Fleig, who operated a Christian retreat in Louisiana, and former state trooper Stephen G. Baggs, a ritual abuse expert, to help prosecute the case.

Sergeant Brown, who had been spearheading the investigation for almost two years at that point, told Lyford that the child molestation accusations and the Kelly Wilson disappearance were not connected, so the Lyford team began considering the possibility that Brown was an accomplice. The Lyford team subsequently got Connie Sue Martin, the thirty-year-old common-law wife of forty-one-year-old Danny Oscar Kerr, to turn state's evidence, and she supposedly filled in some of the blanks in the nine-year-old boy's account and implicated Sergeant Brown.

On the evening of November 7, 1993, seven-year-old Danny Oscar Kerr Jr., the son of Danny Kerr and Connie Sue Martin—and one of the children Child Protective Services had placed in foster care—was taken to the Mitchell County Hospital in Colorado City, Texas, with severe injuries to his upper and lower body and the back of his head. He was quickly flown to Lubbock Methodist Hospital but remained in critical condition. He had fallen into a coma. On November 8, Danny Kerr Jr.'s foster father, fifty-seven-year-old James R. Lappe—who was suspected of causing Danny Jr.'s injuries—shot himself in the head in his Colorado City backyard. On November 10, Lappe's wife, Marie, killed herself as well.

On January 21, 1994, Connie Sue Martin testified before a grand jury. She said that on the final day of Kelly Wilson's life, on or about January 14, Geneva Kerr, the sixty-two-year-old matriarch of the Kerr family, ordered the Kerr men to gang rape Kelly and the Kerr women to sexually molest her and then stabbed Kelly to death herself, cutting off Kelly's breasts. Geneva then reportedly ordered the men to hang Kelly's corpse from a tree so that it could be drained of blood for ritual libations and then butchered for a ritual meal. The Lyford team didn't have a single shred of evidence to substantiate Martin's claims, but the testimony was so shocking that it compelled the grand jury to return indictments. Sergeant Brown and seven members of the Kerr family were subsequently indicted in the disappearance of Kelly Wilson. The seven included sixty-seven-year-old Eugene Wendell Kerr; his wife, Geneva Kerr; their sons, Danny Oscar Kerr and forty-five-year-old Wendell Eugene Kerr, and his thirty-year-old wife, Wanda; forty-four-year-old former Big Sandy and Gilmer police officer Roger Don Holeman; and twenty-five-year-old Tammie Jo Smith. Connie Sue Martin avoided arrest by cooperating with the Lyford team. Sergeant Brown was arrested during a police seminar at Texas A&M University.

The indictments alleged that the defendants kidnapped Kelly Wilson on or about January 5, 1992, confined her at an undisclosed location, raped her repeatedly over a period of several days and then stabbed her to death after a final evening of ritualistic sexual assault and torture.

Kelly Wilson's mother, Cathy Carlson, and her stepdad, Robert Carlson, were shaken to their cores. "Sgt. Brown had become like a member of the family," Cathy said. But special prosecutor Lyford doubled down. He insisted that "the evidence linking Brown to Miss Wilson's case is more than circumstantial" and that the investigation would expose at least four other possible deaths of women and children, but he refused to discuss the details. Bond was set at $250,000 for each defendant regarding the murder charge and $200,000 to $250,000 on each of the additional charges of kidnapping and sexual assault. In addition to this, Holeman and Danny Oscar Kerr were charged with three counts of aggravated sexual assault of a child under fourteen. Sergeant Brown's parents put up their home and property as surety to get their son released on bond.

This shocking turn in the case tore the town of Gilmer apart.

On January 26, 1994, the Kerr property where Wilson was alleged to have been held captive, raped and murdered—all as part of some form of a satanic ritual—was raided, but Lyford team members found nothing to confirm their allegations. To make matters worse, the Gilmer Police Department had no faith in the indictments against Sergeant Brown, and in short order, the Lyford team was no longer working or sharing information with the local police force. In fact, Sergeant Brown had initially been "suspended with pay," and when Mayor Roy Owens changed Brown's status to "suspended without pay," Richard Spruiell, a Gilmer city councilman, Baptist minister and chaplain for the Gilmer Police, resigned his council seat. "I felt the integrity of the mayor's office had been compromised and I wasn't willing to continue serving under those conditions," Spruiell said.

Spruiell didn't stop there. He worked with the Gilmer Police Department to raise $2,300 for Sergeant Brown and his wife's living expenses and shared his opinion of the recent developments in the case freely. "The operative word is *witch hunt*," Spruiell said. "It's very reminiscent of the Salem witch trials. All you have to do is mention the name of someone, and he's arrested and tried."

Gilmer police chief Al McAllister's thoughts mirrored Spruiell's. "I have no problem with arresting a bad officer," McAllister said. "And if he is guilty, I would lead the parade to stone him. But they [the Lyford team] haven't proved to me the man is guilty. I'm confident Sgt. Brown can account for his time on January 14 and I remain unconvinced of the whole thing."

Former Gilmer Baptist minister Richard Spruiell compared the Lyford Team's investigation to a seventeenth-century Salem witch hunt. *Courtesy of the Library Congress.*

Wanda Kerr soon accepted a plea bargain, corroborating all of Connie Sue Martin's claims, save one. She did not implicate Sergeant Brown. And for the moment at least, neither would Cathy Carlson. "For two years, we've been fighting, scratching, pleading for help finding our daughter," she said, "and with the exception of Sgt. Brown, no one helped."

Carlson was also critical of Lyford's professionalism, claiming the special prosecutor explained the gruesome details of how Satanists dispose of bodies while sitting with her in her own living room. "Not only was it tasteless," she said, "but he did not have a shred of evidence." Kelly Wilson's father, Robbie Wilson, of Natchitoches, Louisiana, agreed. "He [Lyford] has given us some vague theories," Mr. Wilson said. "There are some problems with his theories in our minds."

Sergeant Brown insisted that he was innocent from the very beginning, and less than a month after Brown and the Kerrs were indicted, the Lyford team's case against them began to unravel, so much so that many in Gilmer began to view Lyford as the villain—not Brown or the Kerrs. Half the community was even wearing yellow ribbons to support Sergeant Brown.

Reverend Ernie Turney, pastor of the First United Methodist Church in Gilmer, called the entire ordeal an "emotional earthquake." He was worried.

"I sense a lot of pain," he said. "A lot of anxiety…a lot of craziness. And it's coming from many different places. This has become some kind of evil web that has engulfed us all."

On March 7, 1994, the Texas Attorney General's Office took control of the Kelly Wilson case from Scott Lyford and made Assistant Attorney General Shane Phelps the lead prosecutor and investigator. After examining the Lyford team's evidentiary files, Phelps described Lyford's indictments as "a complete and total abandonment of the principles of criminal investigation." On March 14, 1994, the original "emotional earthquake" was followed by a powerful aftershock. Announcing that the evidence the Lyford team had gathered was "insufficient' to support the indictments and further prosecution," the state dropped all of the charges related to the Kelly Wilson disappearance. Sergeant James Brown walked free, but the rest remained in custody on the child molestation charges.

Brown was reinstated with back pay to the Gilmer Police Department two days later, but he didn't return to work immediately. The emotional strain he had suffered since his indictment had clearly taken a toll.

In a letter dated May 6, Lyford team member Deborah Minshew resigned from the Child Protective Services while her recent performance with the agency was under review. According to the *Tyler Morning Telegraph*, the agency's chief of field operations, David Reilly, said officials were afraid that Minshew and Ann Goar "might have been overzealous in their pursuit of a satanic cult that was never proven to exist" and that they "may have disregarded agency policies, resisted oversight and made decisions that may have harmed" the Kerr children, including Danny Kerr Jr. who was still in a coma.

On Wednesday, June 29, 1994, Assistant Attorney General Shane Phelps announced that he and an Upshur County grand jury, which met for almost ten hours, determined that there was no physical evidence supporting the claim that a satanic cult was involved in Kelly Wilson's disappearance, and Phelps criticized the Lyford team. He called the team members "overzealous and inexperienced" and went even further in a prepared statement: "Our review of the Lyford team's interviews of witnesses indicates that their methods of interrogation were overpoweringly suggestive."

Sergeant Brown said that he had no hard feelings toward the grand jury that indicted him, because he believed they were misled. "You will never know what it is like, as an innocent man," he said, "to be faced with the prospect of being executed for something you did not do."

Kelly Wilson's father, Robbie, was pleased with the announcement, even though the investigation was right back where it was before Lyford took over. "We'll start here, pick up the pieces, and we'll get headed in the right direction, hopefully," he said. But Kelly's mother, Cathy Carson, disagreed, reversing her previous stances on the matter. In a three-paragraph statement, Carson was critical of Assistant Attorney General Phelps, complaining that she didn't believe "the findings of Scott Lyford and his investigation team were ever considered, nor taken seriously from the onset."

Cathy Carson and Tami Manos, a spokeswoman for a Justice for Kelly Wilson Committee (previously a clerk for the *Gilmer Mirror*), spent much of the rest of the year defending the Lyford team's findings and taking buses from Gilmer to Austin to protest the Texas attorney general's office, which was then headed by Dan Morales.[87] In December 1994, someone even went so far as to steal a document from the Gilmer Police Department to bolster the committee's stance.

Connie Sue Martin moved to Brooks Fleig's Christian retreat and married. She, Wanda Kerr and the nine-year-old boy who first intimated that he had been a victim of satanic rituals, all later recanted their testimony. The taped interviews of the Lyford team's discussions with Martin were damning. She was not just led and coached but members of the Lyford team also drew up a script to prepare her for her bombshell grand jury testimony. "They told me if I went out and said what they wanted me to say, I wouldn't have no charges against me," Martin said.

The fiasco caused by what the attorney general's office referred to as a "stupid, incompetent and bizarre" investigation of Kelly Wilson's disappearance by the Lyford team "irreparably tainted" the child molestation charges and almost all of them were eventually dropped. On August 24, 1995, after a change of venue, Brent Ward was convicted of aggravated perjury in New Boston. According to the Bowie County court findings, Ward had requested that someone at his place of employment, Holly Lake Ranch, say he was at work the day Kelly Wilson disappeared, but timesheets indicated that Ward hadn't worked that day. According to the *Longview News-Journal*, a coworker, Steve Hedrick, also said that "Ward told him he was worried because Ward and two friends had been at the video store where Wilson worked 15 minutes before the store closed, and that they had been 'messing around with her.'" Hedrick's claims were confirmed by another Holly Lake Ranch employee, John Saladino. He said he heard Ward ask Hedrick to "cover up for him." Ward's legal team appealed the ruling.

In October 1995, Danny Kerr[88] and his former common-law wife, Connie Sue Authement, were relieved of their parental rights by a Bowie County jury. On January 17, 1997, the Sixth Court of Appeals in Texarkana upheld Ward's perjury conviction. Ward moved to Arizona and tried to sue the two attorneys who represented him in the perjury trial for the sum of $80 million in a malpractice suit.

Christopher Denton eventually petitioned for and received a shortened probation period and moved to Arizona. He died of cancer on March 19, 2004. Former Lyford team investigator Ann Goar passed away on August 14, 2007. Connie Sue Authement passed away in Louisiana on March 28, 2017. Brent Ward passed away in the Gilmer area on January 29, 2019.

Sergeant James Brown sued Scott Lyford et al. for the frivolous indictment against him, seeking compensation for severe mental anguish, emotional distress, injury to his good name, personal shame and embarrassment, extreme anxiety and lost earning capacity. He lost the first case and the appeal, because the defendants had operated as representatives of the state and, as such, enjoyed qualified immunity. Brown suffered a series of strokes in late 1994 and was left partially disabled. Early on, the Gilmer Police Department dug up a yard in Gilmer and then part of a larger Upshur County rural property in 1995, but to this day, they still haven't discovered any new clues that might lead to Kelly Dae Wilson's whereabouts.

This much we know: a bright, fun-loving teenager disappeared in Gilmer in 1992, and legitimate efforts to find out what happened to her were tragically transformed into a witch hunt for devil worshippers. And the only reason the story of how the Gilmer community lost track of Kelly Dae Wilson and law enforcement agencies at the local and state levels botched the investigation into her fate isn't more widely known is because another prosecutorial fiasco garnered most of the headlines in those days.

It was the O.J. Simpson trial.

NOTES

Chapter 1

1 *Sulfur* is the usual spelling in American English, but *sulphur*—the preferred spelling in nonscientific texts from outside North America—is used in the tanker's name, so this spelling is used to avoid confusion.

2. The Cuban Missile Crisis was a thirteen-day (October 16–28, 1962) diplomatic confrontation between the United States and the Soviet Union. It was a result of the American discovery of Soviet ballistic missile deployment in Cuba. The confrontation and resulting political showdown are often considered the closest the Cold War came to escalating into a full-scale nuclear war.

3. Confirmed by the March 17, 1964 commandant's action report regarding the Marine Board of Investigation into "the disappearance of the SS *MARINE SULPHUR QUEEN* at sea on or about 4 February 1963 with the presumed loss of all persons on board."

4. The equivalent of $60,000 to $84,000 in 2021.

5. The most recent incident had involved the SS *Pine Ridge*. The T2 tanker broke in two ninety-five miles east of Cape Hatteras on December 21, 1960. The bow section foundered, and seven members of the crew perished. The stern section, however, stayed afloat, and the twenty-nine remaining crew members survived without any serious injuries.

6. For one example, see the March 23, 1964 edition of the *Green Bay Press-Gazette*. It was also referred to as such in the April 1, 1964 *Baytown Sun*.

7. Cofounded in 1948 by Raymond A. Palmer (editor of *Amazing Stories*) and Curtis Fuller, *Fate* is the longest-running magazine devoted to the paranormal. Promoted as "the world's leading magazine of the paranormal," it has published expert opinions and personal experiences relating to UFOs, cryptozoology, mental telepathy, psychic abilities, ghosts and hauntings, strange archaeology, premonitions of death and other paranormal topics.

8. *Argosy*, later titled the *Argosy* and *Argosy All-Story Weekly*, was an American pulp magazine from 1882 to 1978. It is actually considered America's first pulp magazine

9. Some investigators suggest the "mountainous" waves were caused by underwater volcanoes and could get up to two to three hundred feet in height.

10. $172,635 in 1974 is the equivalent of $960,231 in 2021.

Chapter 2

11. New Mexico did not become a state until January 6, 1912.

12. Parker and Turk, "Search for Jessie Evans."

13. John Simpson Chisum (August 16, 1824–December 22, 1884) was a wealthy cattle rancher in the American West during the mid- to late nineteenth century. He was born in Hardeman County, Tennessee, and moved with his family to the Republic of Texas in 1837. Early on, he worked as a building contractor and later served as county clerk in Lamar County. In 1854, Chisum began working at cattle ranching and became one of the first to send his herds to the New Mexico Territory. He procured land along the Pecos River by right of occupancy and became the owner of a large ranch approximately forty miles south of Fort Sumner. Chisum amassed over one hundred thousand head of cattle in short order and eventually entered a partnership with cattlemen Charles Goodnight and Oliver Loving to assemble and drive herds of cattle north to sell to the United States Army in Fort Sumner and Santa Fe, New Mexico, and to provide cattle to miners in Colorado.

14. The Lincoln County War was an Old West conflict between rival factions that began in 1878 in New Mexico Territory, the predecessor of the state of New Mexico, and continued until 1881. The feud became famous because of the participation of the criminal Henry McCarty ("Billy the Kid"). Other notable participants included Sheriff William J. Brady, cattle rancher John Chisum, lawyer and businessman Alexander McSween, James Dolan and Lawrence Murphy.

15. James Joseph Dolan (May 2, 1848–February 6, 1898) was a Union army veteran, cattle rancher, businessman and gunman and a central figure in the Lincoln County War in New Mexico. Dolan was the one who actually hired members of the Jesse Evans Gang (and the John Kinney Gang) to protect his interests.

16. John Henry Tunstall (March 6, 1853–February 18, 1878), a transplanted Londoner, became a rancher and merchant in Lincoln County, New Mexico, where he vied with Irish businessmen, lawmen and politicians who ran the town of Lincoln and the county. Tunstall, who had aspirations of supplanting the Irish and making a fortune as Lincoln County's new boss, was the first man killed in the Lincoln County War.

17. Roberts, *Rangers and Sovereignty*.

18. Hunt, *Tragic Days of Billy the Kid*.

19. Antrim was the last name of Billy the Kid's stepfather.

20. Arizona became a state the month after New Mexico, on February 14, 1912.

21. Eve Ball (March 14, 1890–December 24, 1984) was a teacher and a historian of the American West. She is most well known for her oral history research and works on Apache Native American tribes, particularly *Indeh: An Apache Odyssey*, Eve Ball and Nora Henn, *Indeh: An Apache Odyssey* (Norman: University of Oklahoma Press, 1988).

Chapter 3

22. Andy and Donald were given their stepdad's last name, but Bill Sims never formally adopted them. It was simply a common practice at the time. Their birth father's name was Donald "Ace" Douglass.

23. The Berlin Crisis of 1961 began on June 4, 1961, and lasted until November 9, 1961. It was the last major European incident of the Cold War, and it revolved around the occupational status of Berlin and post–World War II Germany. It started when the USSR communicated an ultimatum demanding the withdrawal of all armed forces from Berlin, including the Western armed forces in West Berlin. The crisis culminated in the Berlin Wall.

24. Former Wichita Falls police officer Charles Edward Trainham passed away on November 9, 2016. He retired thirty years after the Andy Sims disappearance, but he kept a file of the case in his office for the rest of his career.

25. David William Sims would go on to become a member of the influential Austin, Texas noise rock group Scratch Acid, which formed in 1982. He was also a member of Jesus Lizard and performed in several other bands. He continues to play music as of this writing.

Chapter 5

26. *Victoria Advocate*, December 20, 1978.
27. $250 million in 1979 equates to almost $1 billion today.
28. This seizure led to the downfall of the "Cowboy Mafia," based at the Cauble Ranch in Denton, Texas. Cowboy Mafia was the nickname for the most prolific drug smugglers in Texas during the 1970s. Using the shrimp boats *Agnes Pauline*, *Monkey*, *Jubilee* and *Bayou Blues*, the group orchestrated six trips from Colombia to Texas and imported over 106 tons of marijuana from 1977 to 1978.

Chapter 6

29. From Francaviglia, *From Sail to Steam*. A different account indicates that the lone survivor (who the *Dallas Daily Herald* identified as Jim Frisbee) of the *Nautilus* saw Father Verdet get swept overboard. The strewn wreckage along the shore included some dozens of human, horse and cattle corpses. Verdet's body was never recovered.

Chapter 7

30. Kenny Branham also took a lie detector test and passed it.
31. Founded by Daniel M. Eisenberg, the Skip-Tracer Company was a firm employed to find lost persons all over the world.
32. In this context, "White slavery" refers to the largely fictional accounts of White women being abducted and forced into a life of sexual slavery in Mexican brothels across the border.
33. *The Price Is Right* is an American game show where contestants make successive bids on merchandise prizes with the goal of bidding closest to the actual retail price of the prize without going over. The series premiered on NBC's daytime schedule on November 26, 1956, and, at

one time or another, aired in some form across all three of what were then the big three television networks. *The Price Is Right* was one of the only game shows to survive the rigging scandals of the late 1950s and garnered even more popularity after other game shows were exposed for being rigged and cancelled.

34. Constructed in 1934, the Sportatorium, located in downtown Dallas, Texas, was a barn-like arena used primarily for professional wrestling events. The building, which stood at 1000 South Industrial Boulevard, or the intersection of Industrial Boulevard and Cadiz Street, had a seating capacity of approximately 4,500.

35. Whether or not the choice of the Farmer's Branch Police Station instead of a Dallas Police Station was due to Zachary's request is unclear.

36. $25,000 in 1957 is roughly the equivalent of $225,000 in 2021.

37. $16,000 in 1957 is roughly the equivalent of $150,000 in 2021.

Chapter 11

38. According to Brenda McKay, a researcher who works on the missing trio case with Rachel's brother, Rusty Arnold, Renee's jeans had been placed in the trunk and were still there, and the one gift in the car was for Tommy Trlica's son from a previous marriage.

39. Fran Arnold had also contacted Rachel's husband, Tommy, but he was bowling and didn't get to the Seminary South Shopping Mall until much later.

40. For those familiar with the Missing Trio, a scene from *Stranger Things* season one, episode two recalls this heart-wrenching exchange when a frantic, exhausted Joyce Byers (Winona Ryder) hears her son Will say, "Mom?"

41. 1714 West Randol Mill Road is now the address of a Mediterranean restaurant.

42. Not to be confused with Johnnie Swaim, the head coach of Texas Christian University's men's basketball team at the time.

43. $20,000 in 1975 is roughly the equivalent of $95,000 in 2021.

44. She is now known as Walker County Jane Doe. Her murder has never been solved, and her identity has never been established.

45. The Union of Soviet Socialist Republics—also known as the Soviet Union—was a one-party federal socialist state governed by Russia from 1922 to 1991.

Chapter 12

46. Fort Terrett was a U.S. Army post in Sutton County from 1852–1854. Historically referred to as Post on the Rio Llano, Post on the North Fork River Llano and Camp Lugubre, it was named after Lieutenant John Terrett in 1852. Terrett died in the Battle of Monterrey (1846) during the Mexican-American War.
47. *Del Rio News Herald*, July 19, 1987.
48. Simpson, *Cry Comanche*.
49. Rust, "Desperate Fight." Reprinted in *Frontier Times*.
50. Hood, *Advance and Retreat*. Published posthumously.
51. *Emerging Civil War* "John Bell Hood."

Chapter 13

52. Armstrong, "Six Months Old."
53. Ibid.
54. $350,000 in 1956 is roughly the equivalent of $3.35 million in 2021.
55. $1,600 in 1957 is roughly the equivalent of $15,000 in 2021.
56. Margaret—Margaret Tillie Kiefer—left her hometown of Curdsville, Kentucky, in 1929. She left her job at the Hotel Vendome in 1931.
57. There was, after all, a $75,000 estate to settle, which, in the 2020 economy would be $625,000.

Chapter 14

58. Established in 1940 by Ima Hogg, daughter of James Stephen "Big Jim" Hogg (March 24, 1851–March 3, 1906), the twentieth governor of Texas (and the first Texas governor born in Texas). Jim Hogg County is named after him.
59. The equivalent of $133,000 in 2021.
60. All things being equal, Dora Ann Hassell was arguably academically prepared for said oversight. She received a master's degree in education from Colorado State College in 1938 and devoted her thesis to factors underlying the problems girls had with home economics courses in junior high. But things were not equal between the White and Black citizens in the area.

61. John Arthur "Jack" Johnson (March 31, 1878–June 10, 1946), nicknamed the "Galveston Giant," was an American boxer who, at the height of the Jim Crow era, became the first Black world heavyweight boxing champion (1908–1915). Among the period's most dominant champions, Johnson remains a boxing legend, with his 1910 fight against James J. Jeffries dubbed the "fight of the century."

62. A half-renter was a farmer (usually White) who worked and lived on the land of others, paying the landlord half of the money he received for his crops as rent.

63. Letter from Doctor G.J. Hays to J.L. Beaird, the district engineer of Houston County's Highway Department. Hayes was trying to get a marker acknowledging the Slocum Massacre in the mid-1980s.

64. $5,000 in 1910 was the equivalent of $135,000 in 2021.

65. Tim Madigan is an award-winning newspaper journalist and the author of several critically acclaimed books, including *See No Evil: Blind Devotion and Bloodshed in David Koresh's Holy War* (1993) and *The Burning: Massacre, Destruction, and the Tulsa Race Riots of 1921* (2001).

66. As of this writing, Marc Veasey is the United States representative for Texas's thirty-third congressional district, first elected in November 2012.

67. One of the descendants of victims of the Slocum Massacre approached the owner of the property at his fence line a few years ago and entreated the man to let her employ an archaeologist to examine the site with a ground-penetrating radar device, but her request was summarily denied. The man said that up to fifty-five bodies were interred there, but since they were on his property, they were *his* property.

68. The Rosewood Massacre was a racially motivated massacre of Black people and destruction of a Black town that took place during the first week of January 1923 in rural Levy County, Florida. The casualties included at least 6 Black people and 2 White people, though eyewitness accounts suggested a higher death toll of 27 to 150.

69. The Tulsa Race Massacre (also known as the Tulsa Race Riot and the Greenwood Massacre) took place from May 31 to June 1, 1921. White mobs attacked Black residents and businesses of the Greenwood District in Tulsa, Oklahoma. Often called the single worst incident of racial violence in American history, the massacre was carried out on the ground and from private aircraft, destroying more than thirty-five square blocks of the Greenwood district—at that time considered the wealthiest Black community in the United States and referred to as Black Wall Street. A 2001 state commission examination of events was able to confirm thirty-

nine dead, twenty-six Black and thirteen White, based on contemporary autopsy reports, death certificates and other records. The investigation indicated that the overall number of casualties was approximately one to three hundred.

Chapter 15

70. Henry Lee Lucas (August 23, 1936–March 12, 2001) was a convicted American serial killer whose twenty-three-year crime spree began in 1960. He was convicted of murdering eleven people and condemned to death for the murder of Debra Jackson, although his sentence was commuted to life in prison in 1998. Lucas's notoriety grew while he was in prison after he confessed to the Texas Rangers and other law enforcement agencies to more than one hundred murders. He died of congestive heart failure in 2001.

71. Donald Leroy Evans (July 5, 1957–January 5, 1999) was an American serial killer who murdered at least three people from 1985 to 1991. He confessed to killing hundreds of victims at parks and rest areas across more than twenty states.

72. The first Crime Victims Week (later renamed National Crime Victims' Rights Week) was established by President Ronald Reagan in 1981 as a part of an expanding program to provide for victims of crimes (later part of Executive Order 12360, signed in 1982, which created the President's Task Force on Victims of Crime).

Chapter 16

73. A baseball pitcher who prevents the opposing team from achieving one hit is said to have thrown a no-hitter. It is a rare accomplishment for a pitcher or pitching staff. Since 1876, only 303 have been thrown in Major League baseball history. That's an average of about two a year, and pitchers who don't allow a hit over nine innings win more than 99 percent of the time.

74. Some reports say he was a navy pilot; others say he left the navy on December 20, 1945, as electronics technician's mate, first class. Still others claim he served in the Office of Naval Intelligence.

75. *Los Angeles Times*, July 9, 1970.

Chapter 18

76. The equivalent of $1,260,260.

Chapter 19

77. A German-language Treue der Union ("loyalty to the union") monument to the victims of the Nueces Massacre is located in Comfort, Texas. It was dedicated on August 10, 1866.
78. A carpetbagger was a person from the Northern states who went to the South after the Civil War to profit from Reconstruction.
79. Amelia Emaline Moffet passed away in Waverly, Illinois, on January 11, 1904. Her grave is located in the Vancil-Moffet Cemetery in Modesto, Illinois. She is interred alongside her daughter, Aletha Moffet, who passed away in 1876.
80. As the state of Texas has never been keen to claim Unionists, Kansas happily and proudly claims the Moffets, where Dr. Moffet's sons, Alvus and Alva, founded and owned a series of banks.
81. Post-Reconstruction bitterness continued in Bell County well into the twentieth century. On July 22, 1910—just one week before the Slocum Massacre (featured in Chapter 14), the citizens of Belton burned a Black man named Henry Gentry at the stake.
82. *Gaillard's Medical Journal.*
83. *San Saba News*, August 3, 1939.

Chapter 20

84. The travesty of justice in the Timothy Cole case was made exponentially worse by the fact that Cole succumbed to a severe asthma attack in prison ten years before he was cleared posthumously by DNA and the actual perpetrator's confession.
85. Though not a medically recognized malaise, "affluenza" is purported to be a psychological condition affecting wealthy young people.
86. Later known as the West Memphis 3, Baldwin, Echols and Misskelley were convicted of killing the three young boys in 1994 but were freed in 2011 after DNA samples and possible juror misconduct demonstrated that the charges against them were based on insufficient evidence.

87. Daniel C. "Dan" Morales (born April 24, 1956) served as the forty-eighth attorney general of Texas from January 15, 1991, through January 13, 1999, during the gubernatorial administrations of Ann Richards and George W. Bush. As attorney general, Morales procured a $17 billion settlement with big tobacco companies but was later indicted on federal charges for attempting to fraudulently secure hundreds of millions of dollars in attorney fees from the tobacco settlement.

88. Danny Oscar Kerr Sr. passed away on June 5, 2018.

BIBLIOGRAPHY

Abilene Daily Reporter. "Race Riot at Slocum Results in Death of 23 Negroes, 4 Whites." July 31, 1910.

———. "Seven Are Indicted on Murder Charges." August 19, 1910.

Allen, Winnie. "Romance and Adventure in Texas Navy." *Dallas Morning News*, March 13, 1927.

Alto Herald. "East Texas Race Riot, Several Are Killed." August 4, 1910.

———. "Negroes Lynched in Eastern Texas." May 7, 1909.

Amarillo Globe-Times. "Hunt for Girl Hits Dead End." December 2, 1948.

———. "3 Fort Worth Girls Still Missing After 6 Months." June 24, 1975.

Armstrong, Brice. "Six Months Old Today, Patterson Mystery Deepens." *El Paso Herald-Post*, September 5, 1957.

Asbury Park Press. "Mother Keeps 8-year Vigil for Daughter." December 26, 1982.

Austin American-Statesman. "Blood in Plane; Pilot Missing." December 20, 1978.

———. "Civic Leader Hunted, Lost for Four Days." September 28, 1958.

———. "Disappearance of Texas Coed Still Mystery After Six Months." December 2, 1948.

———. "Fant Case Clue Told by Pastor." October 18, 1958.

———. "Lawman Among 8 Charged with Murder." January 24, 1994.

———. "Mrs. Fant Stays Home, Fails to Meet Officer." October 2, 1958.

Baskin, Robert E. "Is Virginia Carpenter Alive?" *Dallas Morning News*, January 18, 1953.

Battista, Arlene. "Facts Revealed in Sikes Case." *Galveston Daily News*, April 5, 1988.

———. "Kidnapping Indictments Returned." *Galveston Daily News*, September 25, 1987.

———. "King's Mother Hears Suicide Notes, Weeps." *Galveston Daily News*, April 7, 1988.

———. "Lawyer Wants King Tapes Suppressed." *Galveston Daily News*, January 28, 1988.

———. "Mother Dreads Anniversary of Shelley's Disappearance." *Galveston Daily News*, May 25, 1988.

———. "Second Trial No Easier than the First." *Galveston Daily News*, June 20, 1988.

———. "Tape Reveals King Confession." *Galveston Daily News*, April 7, 1988.

Baytown Sun. "No One Guessed It Was Voyage to Oblivion." April 1, 1964.

———. "Pilot of Airplane Feared Taken Hostage." December 20, 1978.

———. "Still No Word of Lost Ship." February 10, 1963.

Beaudo, Daren. "Dig Fails to Locate Richerson." *Galveston Daily News*, December 3, 1989.

Bell, Bob Boze. "'I Should Have Killed Them All'—Jesse Evans Gang vs Texas Rangers." *True West*, January 1, 2006.

Berlitz, Charles. *The Bermuda Triangle*. New York: Avon Books, 1974.

Blakely, Mike. "Scoundrel's Luck." *Austin American-Statesman*, September 9, 1986.

Bonham Daily Favorite. "Texas Race Riots; 18 Negroes Killed." August 1, 1910.

Brazosport Facts. "Air Search Continues for Missing Tugboat." November 7, 1966.

Brock, Bob. "Trail of Virginia Carpenter Ends at Doorstep of TSCW Dormitory." *Denton Record-Chronicle*, June 5, 1950.

Bryan Daily Eagle and Pilot. "Anderson County Courthouse Burns." January 7, 1913.

———. "Negro Killers Allowed Bail." May 11, 1911.

———. "Palestine Grand Jury Completes Its Work." August 19, 1910.

———. "Palestine Has Dedicated." September 10, 1910.

———. "13 White Men Held in Jail." August 4, 1910.

———. "Wants Bail for Lynchers." August 3, 1910.

———. "Wants Bail for Lynchers." May 10, 1911.

Charleston Courier. "*San Antonio* Mutiny." April 21, 1843.

Clarridge, Emerson. "'I Didn't Mean to Do It,' Suspect Charged 1974 Killing Say in Interview." *Fort Worth Star-Telegram*, September 26, 2020.

Coast Guard. "M/V *Southern Cities* Disappearance." *Proceedings of the Merchant Marine Council* 25, no. 8 (August 1968): 155–57.

Cochran, Katricia. "Whatever Happened to Andy Sims?" *Fort Worth Star-Telegram*, February 7, 1984.

Commerce Journal. "East Texas Race Riot Several Are Killed." August 5, 1910.

———. "Turned to the Wall." August 5, 1910.

Connelley, William E. *A Standard History of Kansas and Kansans*. Chicago: Lewis Publishing Company, 1918.

Couvillon, Amy. "Investigator Pins Site Where Body May Be Buried." *Galveston Daily News*, April 13, 1990.

———. "Mrs. Doherty Bemoans Lack of Publicity in Case." *Galveston Daily News*, September 10, 1989.

Corpus Christi Caller-Times. "Coast Guard Planes Search for Tanker with 43 Aboard." February 8, 1963.

———. "Expert Rejects Accident Idea." June 21, 1969.

———. "Nine Planes Hunting Missing Boat in Gulf of Mexico." November 7, 1966.

———. "Search for Missing Tug, 6 Crewmen Ends." November 9, 1966.

Cox, Mike. "The Vanishing of *Marine Sulphur Queen*." TexasEscapes.com, June 26, 2014.

Crockett Courier. "Arrested for Shooting." September 7, 1910.

———. "Eight Negroes Killed." July 31, 1910.

———. "Negroes Killed in Anderson County." August 7, 1910.

Cronyn, Ted. "'Freak Sea' Blamed for Loss of Tanker in '63." *Corpus Christi Caller-Times*, June 4, 1969.

Crook, Terri. "State Has No Body, But Feels It Still Has a Case." *Galveston Daily News*, May 29, 1986.

Cuero Record. "The Bermuda Triangle." August 28, 1968.

———. "Seek Son in Killing." June 25, 1965.

Cunningham, Eugene. *Famous in the West*. El Paso: Hicks-Hayward, 1926.

Daily Bulletin (Brownwood). "Trembling Black Rushed onto Street and Hanged." August 1, 1910.

Daily Courier (Connelsville, PA). "Not Race War; Just Slaughter." August 1, 1910.

Daily News-News Telegram. "Hunt Pressed for Missing Texas Youth." December 13, 1961.

———. "Naval Architect Stumped Over Loss of Ship." March 21, 1963.

———. "Search Fails to Find Boy." December 14, 1961.

———. "Witness Says Tanker Loss Proves Puzzle." March 22, 1963.

Daily News (New York). "'Nobody Can Find Us.'" July 4, 1965.

Daily Oklahoman. "Hunt for Missing Texan Futile as 'Leads' Fizzle." August 12, 1962.

Daily Record (Morristown, NJ). "Texas Man May Have Killed More." August 15, 1991.

Dallas Daily Herald. "The *Nautilus*—Further Particulars—A Survivor." September 6, 1856.

Dallas Morning News. "Anderson Quiet; Trouble Seems Over." August 1, 1910.

———. "Assault Trial Postponed for Sanity Test." September 25, 1957.

———. "Birthday Cake Unserved in Gary Bray's Home." August 9, 1955.

———. "Bloodstains on Car Same Type as Fant's." October 1, 1958.

———. "Bond Plea Hearing Set for Zachary." August 28, 1957.

———. "'Boy X' Identified, Definitely Not Gary." August 1, 1955.

———. "Bray Child Sought in Durant Area." July 4, 1955.

———. "Coast Guard Ends Search of Atlantic." February 13, 1963.

———. "Debris Heighten Ship Suspense." February 11, 1963.

———. "Defendant in Assault Out on Bail." November 2, 1957.

———. "East Texas Race Riot, Eighteen Negroes Killed." July 31, 1910.

———. "Fears Grow for Tanker." February 10, 1963.

———. "Five Wives File Damage Suit on Tanker." February 19, 1963.

———. "Gary Disappeared Without a Trace." July 29, 1955.

———. "Human Teeth Found in Field Near Alvin." March 20, 1981.

———. "Insurance Paid to Kin of Men Lost on Tanker." March 6, 1963.

———. "Keller Link Backed." April 10, 1974.

———. "Mate Reveals 2 Groundings of Lost Ship." February 28, 1963.

———. "Missing Child's Description Sent to Philadelphia." March 7, 1957.

———. "Missing Girl Case Remains Unsolved, Says Denton Officer." August 25, 1951.

———. "Mother of Lost Boy in Hospital." July 2, 1955.

———. "Mrs. Fant Stays Home, Fails to Meet Officer." October 2, 1958.

———. "Mrs. Parrack Goes Home." July 8, 1955.

———. "'My Dad's the Greatest' Declares Skipper's Son." February 10, 1963.

———. "Murder Indictment Expected in 27-Year-Old Disappearance Case." November 29, 1984.

———. "National Aid Asked in Search for Gary." July 3, 1955.

————. "No Word Received on Child's Identity." February 24, 1956.

————. "Patterson's Call Related by Witnesses." June 5, 1958.

————. "Police Return to Alvin." March 10, 1981.

————. "Quiet Search Resumed for Bray Baby." August 2, 1955.

————. "Reward Posted for Return of Missing Girl." June 11, 1948.

————. "Sea Mystery Written in Silence." February 17, 1963.

————. "Seven-Year Mystery Unsolved." November 7, 1964.

————. "Sheriff Shy of Clues on Missing Boy." July 7, 1955.

————. "Ship Feared Victim of Disaster at Sea." February 12, 1963.

————. "Ship's Life Ring Seen in Waters Off Miami." February 22, 1963.

————. "*Sulphur Queen* Debris Found by Search Craft." February 21, 1963.

————. "*Sulphur Queen*'s Loss Laid to Blast or Defect." April 14, 1964.

————. "Texas Tanker with 39 Aboard Lost Off Coast." February 9, 1963.

————. "*Time* Ad Hints Family Thinks Fant Still Alive." November 8, 1958.

————. "TSCW Coed Case Widens." August 24, 1957.

————. "Widow's Win Tanker Suit." August 2, 1974.

————. "Zachary Bail Cut to $16,000 in Rape Case." September 9, 1957.

————. "Zachary Test Spurs Inquiry." August 27, 1957.

Del Rio News Herald. "Ceremony to Mark Historic Battle at Devil's River." July 19, 1987.

Denton Record-Chronicle. "Latest Lead in Carpenter Case Proves Fruitless." May 30, 1949.

————. "Missing Girl Case Revived." August 20, 1957.

————. "Philpott Asked About Carpenter; No Link Is Seen." February 5, 1959.

————. "Virginia Carpenter Case 'Lead' Checked." May 23, 1949.

————. "Year-Old Virginia Carpenter Mystery Is Still Unsolved." June 1, 1949.

————. "Zachary Is Quizzed in Carpenter Case." August 23, 1957.

Department of Justice. File No. 152961-1, R.G. 60, 1910.

————. File No. 152961-2, R.G. 60, 1910.

————. File No. 152961-3, R.G. 60, 1910.

Dienst, Alex. "The Second Navy of Texas." *Quarterly of the Texas State Historical Association* 12, no. 20 (October 1909).

Eckhardt, Charlie. "Little Known About Jesse Evans." *Seguin Gazette Enterprise*, April 27, 1994.

El Paso Herald. "Murder and Its Consequences." August 1, 1910.

————. "Ten Negroes Are Killed in Texas Race Riots." July 30, 1910.

El Paso Herald-Post. "After Seven Years—Where Are the Pattersons?" March 2, 1964.

———. "Confusing Questions Unanswered in Patterson Mystery." November 12, 1957.

———. "Patterson Threat Related to Court." May 28, 1964.

———. "Profits Pile Up in Bank for Pattersons." March 15, 1958.

———. "Who Drove Pattersons' Car?" March 14, 1958.

El Paso Times. "El Paso Family's Disappearance Remains Mystery After 60 Years." March 6, 2017.

———. "Still Missing." January 29, 2005.

Emerging Civil War. "John Bell Hood Ambushed at Devil's River." August 8. 2017.

Evening News (Ada, OK). "18 Killed in Race Riot." August 1, 1910.

Farber, James. "Mutiny on the S.A." *Dallas Morning News*, December 2, 1941.

Fort Worth Record. "Bloody Race War at Slocum: Eighteen Negroes Are Killed, No Fatalities Among Whites." July 31, 1910.

———. "Johnson Outclasses Big Jim Jeffries, Negro Is Victor in Fifteenth Round." July 5, 1910.

———. "Race War Ends, State Rangers Make Arrests." August 1, 1910.

———. "Slocum Riot to Be Probed by Grand Jury." August 2, 1910.

Fort Worth Star-Telegram. "All Trails Lead Back to Parking Lot So Far." January 3, 1975.

———. "Bodies of 3 Still Believed in Bayou." April 14, 1975.

———. "Child Toddled into Oblivion 4 Years Ago." September 17, 1959.

———. "Christmas Joy Gone with Girls." December 25, 1975.

———. "Clues Still Scarce on Missing Girls." January 21, 1975.

———. "8-year Quest for Trio Leads Nowhere." December 23, 1982.

———. "Families Ask Help for Girls Via Posters." January 26, 1975.

———. "Families Losing Hope." December 31, 1974.

———. "Families of Three Girls Learn Findings." March 27, 1981.

———. "Families Plead for Return of Missing Girls in Letter." December 29, 1974.

———. "Fate of Missing Girls Remains a Mystery." December 16, 1984.

———. "Five-Year-Old Mystery of Missing Girls Still Haunts Parents." December 24, 1979.

———. "Four Mutineers Hanged in Texas Navy." November 11, 1960.

———. "Grand Jury Works on Riot Cases." August 3, 1910.

———. "Hope Still Alive for Missing Trio." August 10, 1975.

———. "Institutes Probe of Negro Killings." August 2, 1910.

————. "Is He Dead or Walking Distant Streets." December 7, 1958.

————. "Man Denies Link to Missing Trio." August 13, 1975.

————. "Man Held for Obscene Phone Calls May Yield Info on 3 Girls." August 13, 1975.

————. "Missing Girls Letter Discounted by Police." December 25, 1974.

————. "Missing Girls' Mothers Want Nightmare to End." December 23, 1976.

————. "Missing Trio Fails to Come as Call Said." January 8, 1975.

————. "Missing Trio Seen at Mall, Says Friend." January 2, 1975.

————. "Mother Gets Call from Missing Girl." February 8, 1975.

————. "No Leads Reported on Three Missing Girls." December 30, 1974.

————. "No Real Leads Received in Hunt for Three Girls." December 28, 1974.

————. "Note Comes from Missing Girl." December 25, 1974.

————. "Officers, Citizens Hunt for 3 Missing Girls, to No Avail." March 7, 1976.

————. "Police Apprehend Girl Who Made Fake Calls." February 15, 1975.

————. "Police Will Talk to Girls Families." March 28, 1981.

————. "Puzzlement, Anxiety Grow in Case of Missing FW Girls." December 27, 1974.

————. "Race War of Slocum Receives Resolution in Texas House." March 30, 2011.

————. "Reward for Missing Girls Grows by $500 to $4,000." February 10, 1975.

————. "Reward in Case of Missing Girls Now Tops $2,000." January 10, 1975.

————. "Search for Wichita Falls Boy Continues." December 14, 1961.

————. "Search Planned for Missing FW Girls." April 9, 1975.

————. "Search Renewed for Missing Girls, 35 Years After They Vanished." December 23, 2009.

————. "Seven at Palestine Face Murder Charge." August 18, 1910.

————. "Shocking Case Splits Small Town." February 6, 1994.

————. "16 Negroes, 4 Whites Killed in Texas Race Riots Near Palestine." July 30, 1910.

————. "Stolen Plane Found in Gulf City Hangar." December 20, 1978.

————. "Suspect in Boy's Injury Killed Self, Police Say." November 10, 1993.

————. "Talker Quizzed on Missing Man." October 5, 1958.

————. "Tarrant Officers to Check Bones in Brazoria." July 2, 1976.

————. "Three Girls Missing After Shopping Trip." December 24, 1974.

———. "3 Girls Who Vanished from Mall in '74 Haunt Detective's Mind." February 13, 1989.

———. "Trio Missing for Two Weeks." January 7, 1975.

———. "Trio Still Missing after Two Months." February 24, 1975.

———. "Women's Garments Found in Justin Field." January 1, 1975.

———. "Years Bring Few Leads, False Hopes." December 23, 1982.

Francaviglia, Richard V. *From Sail to Steam: Four Centuries of Texas Maritime History, 1500–1900*. Austin: University of Texas Press, 2009.

Frie, Tommy. "Where Is Andy Sims?" *Wichita Falls Times*, December 9, 1968.

Gaddis, Vincent H. "The Deadly Bermuda Triangle." *Argosy*, February 1964.

Gaillard's Medical Journal 44 (1887): 493.

Galveston Daily News. "Area Officers Aid Big Marijuana Bust." December 21, 1979.

———. "Bodies of Two Dickinson Girls Found." April 15, 1981.

———. "Body May Be That of Missing Pilot." December 21, 1979.

———. "Family Hears of Shelley's Final Hour." January 28, 1988.

———. "Friends, Family Attempt to Keep Awareness High." July 7, 1989.

———. "Leads Checked in Pilot Search." December 21, 1978.

———. "Marijuana Vessel Originated Here." December 1, 1978.

———. "More About a Jail Massacre." June 3, 1874.

———. "Reported Sighting of Shelley Sikes Probed." May 29, 1986.

———. "Shelley Sikes Search Comes to Standstill." October 2, 1990.

———. "Sikes Case Reward Offered." May 29, 1986.

———. "Spooky, Small-Town Drama Saga Engulfs Gilmer." February 20, 1994.

———. "Still Waiting." September 10, 1989.

———. "TC Police, FBI Searching for Missing Pilot." December 20, 1978.

———. "Victims of Slocum Mob Were Unarmed." August 1, 1910.

———. "Whites and Blacks Clash, Eighteen Negroes Killed." July 31, 1910.

Gilmer Mirror. "Kelly Wilson Case Remains Unsolved." January 8, 2012.

———. "'Twenty-Year Nightmare.'" January 23, 2013.

Godwin, John. "They Never Came Back from the Hoodoo Sea." *Chicago Tribune*, March 9, 1969.

Green Bay Press-Gazette. "What Happened Aboard Tanker Still Mystery." March 23, 1964.

Green, Felix. *The Piersons and Barnetts of East Texas*. N.p.: self-published, 2013.

Greenville Morning Herald. "Race Riot: Bloodshed." July 31, 1910.

Haisten, Bill. "Missing Girls' Parents Use Radio Talk Show to Question Probes." *Galveston Daily News*, August 24, 1989.

————. "Parents Blast GPD for Probe of Missing Girl." *Galveston Daily News*, August 25, 1989.

Hastings, Karen. "Missionary's Horse Came Back, But He Didn't." *Dallas Morning News*, April 2, 2005.

Hayes, Dr. G.J. "Letter to District Engineer, Texas Highway Dept., October 12, 1984." Houston County Historical Commission.

————. "Letter to Mr. Eliza H. Bishop, March 2, 1984." Houston County Historical Commission.

————. "Letter to Mr. Eliza H. Bishop, April 18, 1984." Houston County Historical Commission.

Holland Evening Sentinel. "Extensive Search Fails to Turn Up Missing Tanker." February 11, 1963.

Hood, John Bell. *Advance and Retreat: Experiences in the United States and Confederate States Armies.* New Orleans: Hood Orphan Memorial Fund, 1880.

Houston Chronicle. "Additional Arrests in Anderson County." August 1, 1910.

————. "Eastern Texas Race War Hot and Bloody. July 31, 1910.

————. "Judge Gardner's Court Is Rushing Investigation." August 2, 1910.

————. "The Man Hunt Is Denounced." August 2, 1910.

————. "No Indictments Are Found in Palestine." August 15, 1910.

————. "13 White Men Held in Jail." August 3, 1910.

————. "21 Negroes Are Dead, 3 White Men Wounded." July 30, 1910.

Hunt, Frazier. *The Tragic Days of Billy the Kid.* Santa Fe, NM: Sunstone Press, 2009.

Kilgore News Herald. "Missing Man Believed Seen." October 17, 1958.

————. "No Clues Found in Fant Case After Two Months." November 24, 1958.

————. "Paper Say Officer Part of Assault." February 11, 1994.

Kirkpatrick, Joe. "Skull Discovered on Bank of Canal." *Galveston Daily News*, October 31, 1989.

Kleinberg, Eliot. "Texas Ranger Will Take Mystery to Grave." *Seguin Gazette-Enterprise*, July 17, 1985.

Laird, Cheryl. "Investigators in Richerson Case Open Up." *Galveston Daily News*, July 28, 1989.

Loe, Victoria, and Alan Pusey. "Gilmer Witness Coached on the Story, Tapes Show." *Dallas Morning News*, August 28, 1994.

Lomax, John Nova. "Houston 101: A Notorious Montrose Murder's (Alleged) Connection to the Deaths of JFK and MLK." *Houston Press*, August 6, 2009.

Longview News-Journal. "Discovered Bones Not Those of Missing Girl." June 12, 2002.

———. "Missing: Retired Ranger Still Searching for Woman." July 14, 1985.

———. "Whatever Happened to Andy?" January 1, 2009.

Lopez, Meghan. "Few Answers Sixty Years After El Paso Couple Disappeared." KFOX, February 17, 2017.

Los Angeles Times. "Slaying of Two in 1965 Still a Mystery." July 9, 1970.

Lubbock Avalanche-Journal. "Board Recesses Inquiry in Boat's Disappearance." December 1, 1966.

Lubbock Morning Avalanche. "Last Man to See Missing Coed Is Charged in Assault Attempt." August 20, 1957.

Madigan, Tim. "A Century Later, Texas Race Massacre Forgotten by All but a Few." *Fort Worth Star-Telegram*, February 20, 2011.

———. "Story of Slocum Massacre of 1910 'Needs to be Told.'" *Fort Worth Star-Telegram*, February 27, 2011.

Marshall News Messenger. "Alabama Officers Deny Etex Negro Attack Story." February 5, 1959.

Marten, James. *Texas Divided: Loyalty & Dissent in the Lone Star State, 1856–1974.* Lexington: University of Kentucky Press, 1990.

Mashek, John. "Rape Attempt Case Revives '48 Missing Girl Investigation." *Dallas Morning News*, August 20, 1957.

Miami Herald. "Witnesses Tell of Fright Aboard Tugboat Lost in Gulf Storm." November 30, 1966.

Michno, Gregory. *Encyclopedia of Indian Wars: Western Battles and Skirmishes, 1850–1890.* Missoula, MT: Mountain Press, 2003.

Miller, Brian Craig. *John Bell Hood and the Fight for Civil War Memory.* Knoxville: University of Tennessee Press, 2010.

Miller, Rick. *Bloody Bell County: Vignettes of Violence and Mayhem in Central Texas.* Waco, TX: Eakin Press, 2011.

Monitor (Brownsville, TX). "Circuit-Riding Padres Tell Early Valley Tales." March 16, 1969.

Mueller, Thomas. "Officers Search for Woman." *Galveston Daily News*, May 27, 1986.

mySA. "Texas Family Seeks to Solve 42-year Long Mystery." December 10, 2016.

Natchez Weekly Courier. "Mutiny on Board the Texan Schooner-of-War *San Antonio*." April 12, 1843.

New York Times. "Calvary to Quell Outbreak in Texas." August 1, 1910.

———. "Fifty May Be Dead in Texas Race Riots." July 31, 1910.

———. "More Texas Riot Arrests." August 7, 1910.

———. "Scores of Negroes Killed by Whites." July 31, 1910.

Nieman, Robert. *Texas Ranger Hall of Fame E-Book*. Waco: Texas Ranger Hall of Fame and Museum, 1994.

Odessa American. "Elderly Woman May Have Seen Kidnapping." March 14, 1975.

———. "Search for 3 Missing Girls Is Scheduled." April 10, 1975.

Okada, Bryon. "Denton Digs into Mystery of Woman's Disappearance." *Fort Worth Star-Telegram*, July 7, 1998.

———. "Search of Denton Dam Is Halted with No Sign of Woman's Remains." *Fort Worth Star-Telegram*, July 9, 1998.

Orange Leader. "Satanic Cult Suspected of Raping, Killing Teen." January 23, 1994.

Overton, Mac. "Case Worker Planned to Target Chief Deputy." *Gilmer Mirror*, August 6, 1994.

———. "Fabricated Testimony Alleged in CPS Cases." *Gilmer Mirror*, August 6, 1994.

Paddock, Buckley B., comp. *A History of Central and Western Texas*. Vol. 2. Chicago: Lewis Publishing, 1911.

Palestine Daily Herald. "All Quiet at Slocum." August 2, 1910.

———. "Carried to Crockett." August 22, 1910.

———. "Seven Men Are Indicted on Charge of Murder." August 18, 1910.

———. "Situation in Hand, the Law Effective." August 1, 1910.

———. "Three Men Liberated." August 13, 1910.

———. "Venue Is Changed to Harris County." December 14, 1910.

———. "Whites and Negroes in Serious Conflict." July 30, 1910.

Paris News. "Missing Girls Sought Here." January 29, 1975.

Parker, Rick, and David S. Turk. "The Search for Jessie Evans." *Wild West*, August 2009

Parker, Vic. "Kelly Wilson: The Search Continues." *Longview News-Journal*, January 5, 1997.

Pensacola News. "Note in Bottle? Reality or Hoax?" May 21, 1963.

Press and Sun-Bulletin. "Texas Family Carries on Hunt for Daughter Missing 8 Years." December 23. 1982.

Record (Hackensack, NJ). "Jackets Found, But Fate of Ship Still Is Mystery." February 21, 1963.

Rigler, Lewis. *In the Line of Duty: Reflections of a Texas Ranger Private*. Denton: University of North Texas Press, 1995.

Ritzman, Marlene, and Stanley N. Moffet. *Moffat, Texas: A History*. Larned, KS: N.p., 1984.

Roberts, Dan W. *Rangers and Sovereignty*. San Antonio, TX: Wood Printing & Engraving Co., 1914.

Rossen, Jake. "Cold Case: Revisiting Houston's Infamous Ice Box Murders." *Mental Floss*, November 4, 2019.

Rubin, Bernard. "Mysterious Disappearance of Carpenter Girl Unsolved." Denton Record-Chronicle, January 30, 1949.

Rust, Herman G. "Desperate Fight on Devil's River." *Frontier Times* 21, no 4 (January 1944), 140–43.

Sadler, Jerry, and James Neyland. *Politics, Fat-Cats & Honey-Money Boys*. Santa Monica, CA: Roundtable Publishing, 1984.

San Saba News. "Mrs. Hattie Grimes Answers Call Sat., July 29." August 3, 1939.

Semi-Weekly Courier-Times (Tyler, TX). "Galveston Negro Knocked Out Jeffries in Fifteenth Round." July 6, 1910.

———. "Grand Jury Begins Work on Negro Killing Cases." August 3, 1910.

———. "Race Riot Reported at Slocum, Anderson Co." July 31, 1910.

———. "The White Men Now Confined." August 13, 1910.

Shreveport Journal. "Intense Hunt Continues for Dallas Child." July 1, 1955.

"Significant Case." *DEA World* 4, no. 11 (1979).

Simon, Janice. "Families Mark Painful Anniversaries." *Galveston Daily News*, October 5, 1990.

———. "Search Resumes for Shelley Sikes." *Galveston Daily News*, September 26, 1990.

Simpson, Harold B. *Cry Comanche: The 2nd U.S. Cavalry in Texas, 1855–1861*. Hillsboro, TX: Hill Jr. College Press, 1979.

South Florida Sentinel. "Missing Juvenile." October 8, 1992.

Stanton, Robert. "Sikes Case May Be Solved." *Galveston Daily News*, June 29, 1987.

———. "Unsolved Murders: No Arrests Made in at Least 25 County Homicides." *Galveston Daily News*, September 20, 1987.

Tampa Bay Times. "Four-Year Old Sea Mystery Still Unsolved." May 1, 1967.

Telegraph and Texas Register. "Mutiny and Murder on Board the *San Antonio*." February 23, 1842.

Thomas, Kathy. "Residents Cautious After Abduction." *Galveston Daily News*, June 4, 1986.

Thorpe, Helen. "Historical Friction." *Texas Monthly*, October 1997.

Time. "Investigations: The Queen with the Weak Back." March 8, 1963.

Times Record (Troy, NY). "Mystery at Sea." April 16, 1964.

Times Record News. "Case of Missing 11-Year-Old Unsolved After 47 Years." December 6, 2008.

Times-Picayune (New Orleans). "The Loss of the *Nautilus*." August 26, 1856.

―――. "12 Nabbed in Pot Bust on Texas Shrimp Boat." December 1, 1978.

Tyler Courier-Times. "Kelly Wilson Rumors Fly Around ET." April 25, 2004.

Tyler, George W. *History of Bell County (1936).* Belton, TX: Dayton Kelley, 1966.

Tyler Morning Telegraph. "AG's Office: Brown Innocent." June 30, 1994.

―――. "Dutch Ship May Have Seen *Sulphur Queen*." March 27, 1963.

―――. "Eight Arraigned in Teen's Death." January 24, 1994.

―――. "Four Years and Counting." January 5, 1996.

―――. "Gilmer Man Reindicted for Perjury." October 28, 1993.

―――. "Gilmer Man Turns Self in to Sheriff." September 1, 1993.

―――. "Gilmer Social Worker Resigns." May 18, 1994.

―――. "Holidays Interrupt Kelly Wilson Search." December 22, 1995.

―――. "Kelly Wilson Case Suspect Subpoenaed." January 25, 1995.

―――. "Lack of Evidence Cited in Wilson Case." March 15, 1994.

―――. "Missing Gilmer Teen's Case Shows Need for Regional Coordination." July 26, 1992.

―――. "Organizers, Crowd Seek 'Justice for Kelly Wilson.'" August 22, 1994.

―――. "Suspect in Kelly Wilson Disappearance Declines Upshur County Grand Jury Appearance." January 28, 1995.

―――. "Suspect in Missing Girl Case Says He Was Abducted." January 22, 1993.

―――. "Suspended Gilmer Officer Accepts Reinstatement." March 17, 1994.

―――. "Teen Arrested for Slashing Missing Girl's Tires." July 26, 1992.

―――. "Wilson Case Drama Unfolds Daily." January 27, 1994.

Vargo, Joe. "Looking for Shreds of Hope." *Austin American-Statesman*, October 14, 1988.

Victoria Advocate. "Charter Plane's Pilot Object of Police Hunt." December 20. 1978.

―――. "Family Puts Marker on Empty Grave of a Missing UT Student." May 24, 1996.

―――. "Lawmen Grill Lucas About Local Murders." December 20, 1984.

―――. "Officers in Port Continue Probe." April 23, 1981.

―――. "Police Seek Information." April 11, 1981.

———. "Port Housewife Still Missing After Year." August 29, 1979.

———. "Port Woman Sought." September 6, 1978.

———. "Port Woman Still Missing." October 13, 1978.

———. "Whereabouts Remain Mystery." April 14, 1981.

Waco News-Tribune. "Waco Police Asked to Join Search for Missing Co-Ed." June 9, 1948.

Waco Tribune-Herald. "Sea Widows Get Damages from 1963." August 2, 1974.

Wade, Ronald M. "When Satan Came to Texas: A Study in a Satanic Panic Witch Craze." *Skeptic* 7, no. 4 (Fall 1999), 40–44.

Washington (IN) *Herald.* "Deaths Result from Race Riots." July 6, 1910.

———. "Fearful Toll in Texas Riot." August 1, 1910.

Washington Post. "Condemns Texas Slayers." August 8, 1910.

Watt, Chad Eric. "Service to Mark Anniversary of Tragedy." *Galveston Daily News,* May 24, 1996.

Welch, Linda Latham. "Hope, Despair Haunts Parents of Lost Woman." *Austin American-Statesman,* October 21, 1988.

Wichita Falls Times. "Boy Is Missing Here for 12 Years." December 9, 1973.

———. "Four-Year Hunt for Boy Pushed." December 9, 1965.

———. "Helicopter Aids Hunt for Missing Sims Boy." December 14, 1961.

———. "Missing Andy Sims Is City's Most Puzzling Case." June 24, 1962.

Williams, Scott E. "Bone Pieces Might Belong to Missing Woman, Police Say." *Galveston Daily News,* December 5, 1998.

———. "Police to Announce Results of Richerson Search." *Galveston Daily News,* December 4, 1998.

INDEX

ABOUT THE AUTHOR

Award-winning writer E.R. Bills is the author of *Texas Obscurities: Stories of the Peculiar, Exceptional and Nefarious* (The History Press, 2013); *The 1910 Slocum Massacre: An Act of Genocide in East Texas* (The History Press, 2014); *Black Holocaust: The Paris Horror and a Legacy of Texas Terror* (Eakin Press, 2015); *Texas Far & Wide: The Tornado With Eyes, Gettysburg's Last Casualty, The Celestial Skipping Stone and Other Tales* (The History Press, 2017); and *The San Marcos 10: An Antiwar Protest in Texas* (The History Press, 2019).

Bills has also written for the *Austin American-Statesman*, the *Fort Worth Star-Telegram*, *Texas Co-Op Power* magazine and *Fort Worth Weekly*. He currently lives in North Texas with his wife, Stacie.

Visit us at
www.historypress.com